# LOST SUWANNEE COUNTY

# LOST SUWANNEE COUNTY

ERIC MUSGROVE

THE History PRESS

Published by The History Press
Charleston, SC
www.historypress.net



*Front cover*: State Archives of Florida.
*Back cover, top*: State Archives of Florida; *bottom*: State Archives of Florida.

First published 2017

Manufactured in the United States

ISBN 9781625858238

Library of Congress Control Number: 2017934936

*To Sarah, Alex and Abby, for putting up with my hours away from them,*
*and for those in Suwannee County who have come before me…*

# CONTENTS

# ACKNOWLEDGEMENTS

I would like to thank all those who have helped in this project, and doubtless I will forget some. First of all, my family for their support and understanding during the many hours I was holed up in my home office researching and typing. A special thanks to my wife, Sarah, who as usual has provided her support for my writing as well as proofing the text.

Also, for those in Suwannee County's history who took the time to photograph or write down what transpired, allowing future historians such as myself the chance to learn just a little bit about what they faced during their lives. I must also thank the Suwannee County Clerk of Court's Office for making it possible for the public to see firsthand the records that cover so many facets of our county's history. The Suwannee County Historical Commission and the Suwannee County Historical Museum have also preserved many photographs, documents and items that show the history of our citizens. The Photographic Collection of the State Archives of Florida is a wonderful central repository of thousands of documents and photographs that have been helpful in the completion of this work.

I must thank my assistant Logan Woods, who on her own time performed research, pored over my manuscript and offered many suggestions. I must not neglect the many citizens who, knowing my love of history, have dropped off photographs, documents and stories that have expanded my knowledge of Suwannee County.

I must also thank my acquisitions editor, Amanda Irle, and copy editor, Rick Delaney, for their working with me during the months that it took to prepare this work for print.

I could not have done it without all of you.

# INTRODUCTION

The birth of Suwannee County took place on December 21, 1858, when the Florida legislature carved out the western portion of Columbia County. However, its history spans long before that time. Whether it was the Native Americans, the Spanish or others who lived in the area before the Americans arrived, they each have made their mark on the county's history. The natural springs of the Suwannee River in locations such as Lower Mineral Spring (now Suwannee Springs) and elsewhere brought health resorts to Suwannee County.

Suwannee County came of age during the Civil War when many of its men went off to serve. The citizens left behind did their best to continue life as normal, working in the fields and providing essential government services. Some citizens made their mark on the war, including Live Oak native Lewis Thornton Powell, who was involved in the Lincoln assassination. The end of the war saw a changed lifestyle for many Suwannee County citizens as slavery was outlawed throughout the United States. The county grew after the war as citizens from all over the country flocked to the pristine waters and virgin timber of the area. Railroads began to dot the landscape as free men and convicts alike worked in the natural resources. By the first years of the twentieth century, such economic opportunities had made the county seat of Live Oak the fifth-largest city in the state of Florida.

However, a devastating boll weevil attack during World War I crippled Suwannee County's cotton production, and it took years to find another cash crop to replace it. Meanwhile, central and south Florida were growing

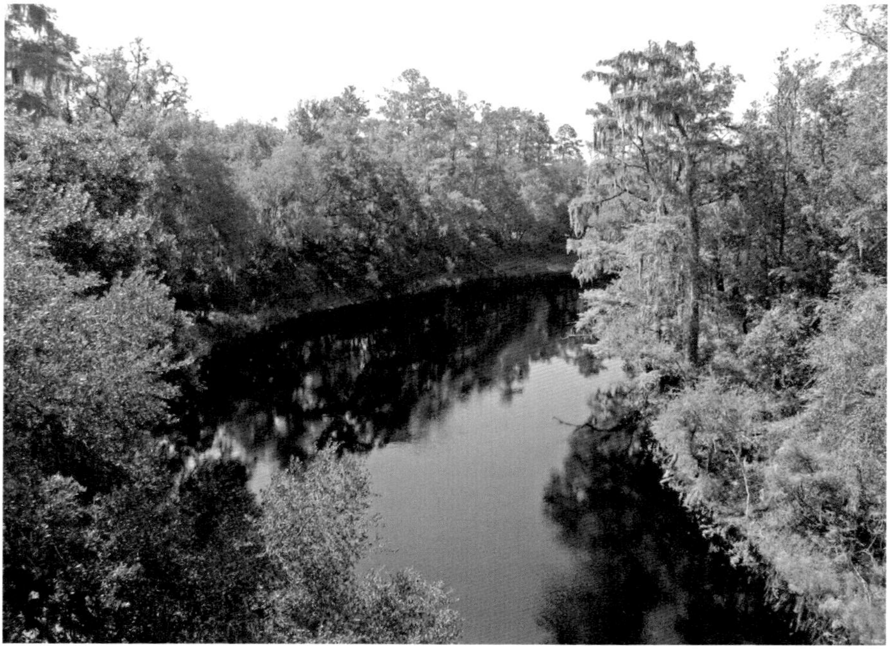

The Suwannee River gently meanders through south Georgia and north Florida, as it has done for countless ages. It is seen here around 2000. *United States Geological Survey.*

exponentially as citizens relaxed at the beaches and health resorts located there, leaving places such as Suwannee Springs as they realized the sulfur waters had no cleansing effects. Coupled with the Great Depression, Suwannee County's growth slacked off as farmers struggled to make ends meet. Many communities withered or died as their citizens moved to more profitable areas of the country. The county's political clout, however, remained strong.

World War II brought some growth into the county as Florida benefited from war production and training. After the war, the county lost much of its statewide political influence as legislative boundaries were modified to incorporate the drastic growth of central and south Florida. Agriculture continued to remain the most robust economic value Suwannee County had to offer. The rise of ecotourism within Florida has now led to a major boom in Suwannee County as people visit the numerous springs or canoe down the majestic and gently meandering Suwannee River.

The history of Suwannee County, invariably linked forever with being "way down upon the Swanee River," has seen its fair share of interesting moments. Some of those moments are remembered by the local population, used as marketing promotions for those who visit Suwannee County or incorporated into the many historic buildings that dot the landscape.

Other historical moments, however, have long been forgotten. Found in dusty attics, county archives or other locations, these historical gems are sometimes even more interesting than well-known aspects of Suwannee County's history. From former ways of living to presidential assassins to wives of famous pilots (and everything in between), this lost history, as it were, has helped to define Suwannee County and its inhabitants. It is for these lost memories that this work is written.

# PART I

# FORGOTTEN PEOPLE AND EVENTS

# 1
# PRESIDENTIAL CONSPIRATOR

## *Lewis Thornton Powell*

If you look long enough in any locale's history, you will find that there are good parts of history as well as bad. As some have said, "History is what it is; we can't change it." Or, as someone else once said, "Those who don't know the past are doomed to repeat its mistakes." Such is the case with young Lewis Thornton Powell.

Powell was born in Randolph County, Alabama, in 1844, the youngest of eight children of George C. Powell, a Baptist minister, farmer, blacksmith and schoolteacher. When Lewis was three, his father moved the family to Georgia, where they resided until 1859. In that year, George Powell moved the family to a site just outside of Live Oak in recently established Suwannee County; Lewis was fifteen at the time.

Lewis was a quiet, introverted youth. However, he did love to care for animals, and he was quickly nicknamed "Doc" because of his fondness for nursing animals back to health. Lewis was a rather tall and rugged lad, standing six feet, four inches. His rugged look only increased when he was kicked in the jaw by a family mule at the age of twelve or thirteen. The jaw healed, but the left side became more pronounced than the right; it was a trait that Lewis would have until his death.

When the Civil War began in 1861, Lewis was only seventeen years old. Quickly siding with the Confederacy, he enlisted in Jasper with the Hamilton Blues, later known as Company I of the Second Florida Infantry Regiment. The Hamilton Blues were made up of men from Hamilton, Suwannee and surrounding counties. The Second Infantry Regiment fought throughout

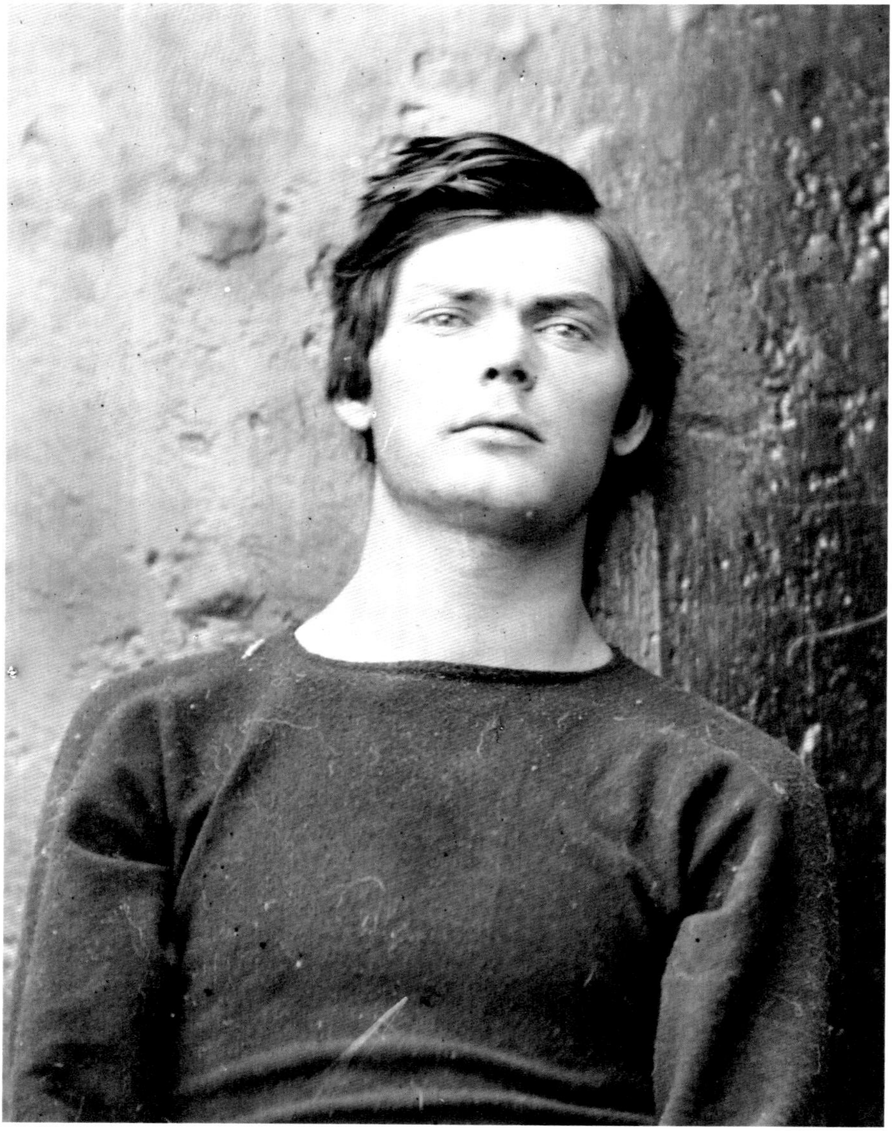

Lewis Thornton Powell at the age of twenty-one, in 1865. *Suwannee County Clerk of Court.*

1862 and 1863, including at the Seven Days Battles around Richmond, Sharpsburg (also known as Antietam), Fredericksburg and Chancellorsville. After the Battle of Sharpsburg, the Second Florida became one of three infantry regiments that constituted the Florida Brigade led by Brigadier

General Edward Perry (and usually known as Perry's Brigade). Lewis remained unwounded until the pivotal Battle of Gettysburg in July 1863, when he was injured and captured the day before his unit participated in the famous but failed Pickett's Charge on the third day of the battle. Lewis was not alone, as 65 percent of the Florida Brigade's men were killed, wounded or captured in the battle, the highest casualty rate of any Confederate brigade at Gettysburg. Eventually, Lewis was transferred to Baltimore, Maryland, as a prisoner of war to recuperate from his wounds. While there, he befriended a female nurse who probably helped him escape a week after his arrival. Lewis fled to Confederate lines in nearby Virginia.

Unable to find his own infantry regiment, Lewis joined the Forty-Third Battalion of the Virginia Cavalry, better known as Mosby's Rangers, a Confederate cavalry unit with a history of guerrilla tactics. The battalion would make swift raids behind Union lines to destroy supply trains and disrupt Union communications, then return to their bases and melt into the general population. The North hated the Rangers because they tied up some seventeen thousand Northern troops who could have been used elsewhere (not a bad ratio for a group that usually had no more than four hundred men). Lewis fit in well with Mosby's Rangers, and they found him to be eager, ready for battle, generous, chivalrous and a gentleman. Lewis left the Forty-Third Battalion in January 1865 after possibly joining the Confederate Secret Service in the fall of 1864. Returning to Baltimore, he lodged in the boardinghouse of the nurse who had probably helped him to escape in 1863. Lewis was charged with beating a black maid but was released when a witness failed to appear. Required to sign an oath of allegiance, he signed it as "Lewis Paine"; he had boarded with a Payne family while part of Mosby's Rangers and apparently spelled the name phonetically.

While in Baltimore, Powell was introduced to the famous actor and devoted Confederate John Wilkes Booth, who planned to kidnap President Abraham Lincoln and hold him in exchange for Confederate prisoners. As the Civil War ended, the plan evolved into an assassination attempt on not only Lincoln but also Vice President Andrew Johnson and Secretary of State William Seward. Young Lewis Powell was given the responsibility of assassinating Seward, who had recently been involved in a carriage accident and was recuperating nearby. On April 14, 1865, as Booth shot Lincoln during a performance of *Our American Cousin* at Ford's Theatre, Powell went to the house in which Seward was recuperating and gained entrance as a doctor's delivery boy. Within minutes, he had wounded five men, including Seward and two of his sons, and then fled the scene. The secretary of state survived only because he had a splint around his jaw from his recent carriage accident that deflected Powell's knife; as it was, Seward was left with major permanent scars on his face. Only Booth and Powell performed their "mission"; the other conspirators failed to act.

Powell escaped to a cemetery after taking a wrong turn, but he was captured two nights later when he appeared at the doorsteps of one of the other co-conspirators, Mary Surratt, just as she was being arrested. Powell's story that he was there to clean out gutters in the middle of the night did not help him, nor did Surratt's denial of ever knowing him, as he was recognized by one of William Seward's aides. During the ensuing trial, Powell was found to be stoic, dignified and chivalrous, and the press published more on him than on any of the others save Mary Surratt. Found guilty, Powell went to the gallows on July 7, 1865, along with fellow conspirators Surratt, David Herold and George Atzerodt. To his dying breath, Powell pleaded for Surratt's life, stating that she was innocent of the charges. Powell, who at twenty-one was the youngest of the conspirators, was the last to die. He was buried in a cemetery near the gallows.

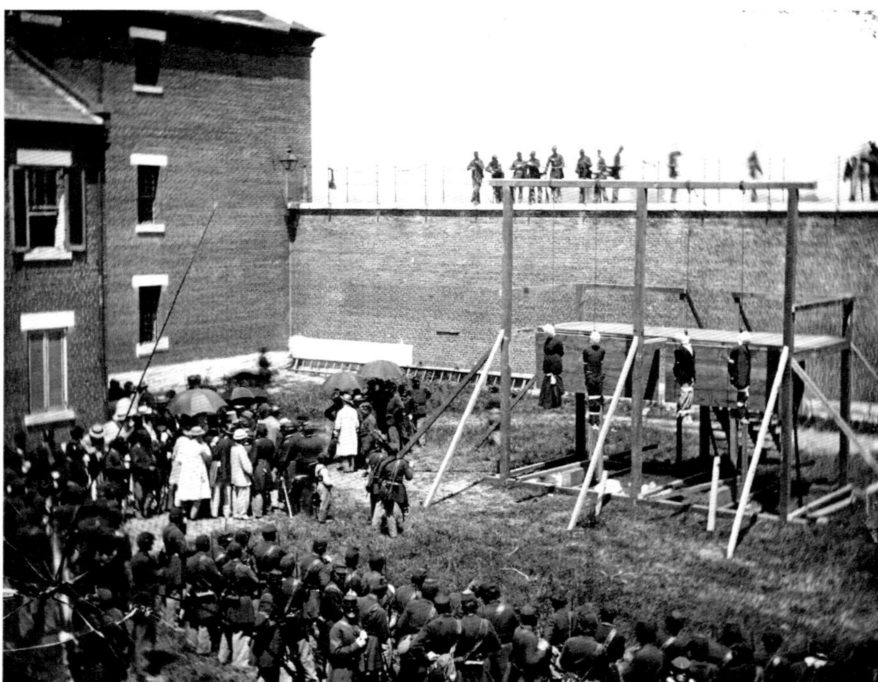

Lewis Powell and other Lincoln conspirators going to the gallows in July 1865. *Suwannee County Clerk of Court.*

George Powell, still living in Live Oak, supposedly tried to make it to Washington, D.C., for his son's trial and execution, but illness kept him home. More than a year after Lewis Powell's hanging, the surviving members of the Powell family moved from Live Oak into what is now Seminole County (George C. Powell's last confirmed marriage in Suwannee County was on September 3, 1866, based on county marriage books). It is probable that the stigma of having a son associated with Lincoln's assassination, or threats received due to his son's involvement, was too much for George Powell in Reconstruction-era Suwannee County. Or, perhaps he saw greater chances for evangelism in the relatively unpopulated counties to the south. Whatever the case, the Powell family remained in central Florida.

In an odd twist of fate, Lewis Powell's skull was lost for over 120 years until a search in the anthropology department of the Smithsonian Institution found a young white male's skull mixed with numerous Native American ones. The number 2244 on the skull referred to the "Cranium of Lewis Payne, Hung at Washington City for Complicity in the Assassination of Abraham Lincoln." In 1994, the skull was returned to the family and interred next to George C. Powell's remains in Seminole County.

2

# POLITICS AS USUAL

## *The Selection of the County Seat*

There are events in the history of Suwannee County that may remind you of the passage from Ecclesiastes 1:9, in which the wise King Solomon declares, "What has been is what will be, and what has been done is what will be done, and there is nothing new under the sun." The selection of Live Oak as the county seat is one such event, involving twisted politics, bribery, blackmail and other illegal activities.

When Suwannee County was created on December 21, 1858, the original designated county seat was "the house of William Hines" until more permanent facilities could be located. Hines was county judge and owner of twenty-four slaves who owned property north of present-day Live Oak in the Antioch area. It was obvious that his home was only a stopgap measure until the county could decide on better accommodations.

Elections were held in April 1859 to elect a clerk of the circuit court, sheriff, coroner, county surveyor, assessor and collector of taxes, judge of probate (who was also county judge) and four county commissioners. Houston (pronounced "house-ton"), one of only two or three decent-sized communities in Suwannee County and located in the northeast quarter of the county, became the first permanent seat sometime in 1859. By the fall of 1859, county records were being written there. These records were probably created on a portion of the eighty acres that were purchased by the county commissioners on the south side of the Pensacola & Georgia Railroad line (near the current Suwannee County Country Club and Camp Weed). An order by Circuit Court Judge James M. Baker in circuit court minutes from

January 1860 states that a suitable courthouse had been erected in Houston, and he revoked the order to hold court in the house formerly owned by William Hines.

Around the same time that Houston was established, the Pensacola & Georgia Railroad passed a particularly large live oak tree several miles to the west. This large tree shaded a pond, and many settlers used the tree and pond in passing. When the railroad was being built through the area just before the Civil War, the workers would rest in the shade of the tree and eat their meals. After the railroad's completion, a depot was established near the tree; the community that sprang up around it was aptly named Live Oak. During the war, the community began to grow, especially after a railroad junction was established there leading into Georgia. This connection brought in more settlers; soon after the Civil War ended, Live Oak was larger than Houston.

One of those settlers was John Parshley, who in 1866 arrived from Ohio and settled in Live Oak. He constructed a large two-story home across the street from the present courthouse after his wife, Nancy, and their six children moved there in 1867. John Parshley laid out many of the downtown streets that are still used today, and he established a large sawmill and planing mill on the block north of the current First Baptist Church.

As a result of Live Oak's more central location and heavy politicking by John Parshley and others, the Florida legislature named the community as

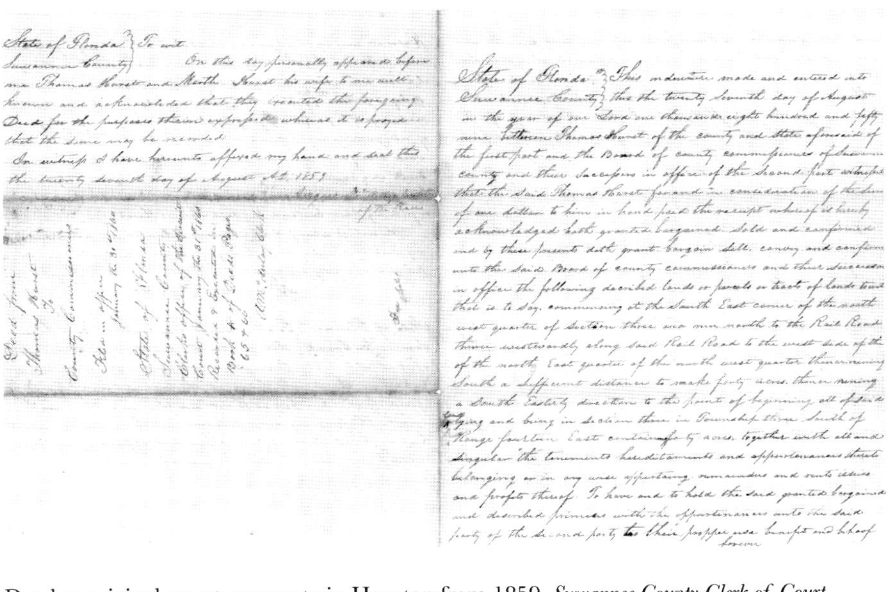
State of Florida } To wit
Suwannee County } On this day personally appeared before me Thomas Hurst and Martha Hurst his wife to me well known and acknowledged that they executed the foregoing Deed for the purposes therein expressed whereas it is prayed that the same may be recorded
In witness I have hereunto affixed my hand and seal this the twenty seventh day of August AD 1859

State of Florida } This indenture made and entered into
Suwannee County } this the twenty seventh day of August in the year of our Lord one thousand eight hundred and fifty nine between Thomas Hurst of the county and State aforesaid of the first part and the Board of county commissioners of Suwannee county and their successors in office of the second part witnesseth that the said Thomas Hurst for and in consideration of the sum of one dollar to him in hand paid the receipt whereof is hereby acknowledged hath granted bargained sold and confirmed and by these presents doth grant bargain sell convey and confirm unto the said Board of county commissioners and their successors in office the following described lands or parcels or tracts of lands to wit that is to say commencing at the South East corner of the north west quarter of Section three and run north to the Rail Road thence westwardly along said Rail Road to the west side of the of the north East quarter of the north west quarter thence running South a sufficient distance to make forty acres thence running a South Easterly direction to the point of beginning all of said lying and being in Section three in Township three South of Range fourteen East containing forty acres together with all and singular the tenements hereditaments and appurtenances thereto belonging or in any wise appertaining remainder and rents issues and profits thereof To have and to hold the said granted bargained and described premises with the appurtenances unto the said party of the second party to their proper use benefit and behoof forever

Deed to original county property in Houston from 1859. *Suwannee County Clerk of Court.*

the county seat on August 1, 1868. Unfortunately for John Parshley, he would die a week later from what was most probably malaria; at the time, Live Oak was full of ponds and swamps. The move of the county seat from Houston to Live Oak appears to have been done quickly and rather smoothly, as the last records dated from Houston are from the last week of July and the first in Live Oak are dated the first week of August. However, the selection of the specific permanent site for the county courthouse did not go as smoothly.

Once the state legislature decided that Live Oak would be the county seat on August 1, 1868, it was up to the local government to determine exactly where the courthouse would be located. Changes in Florida laws now required that the county commissioners keep minutes of their actions; this fortunate decision provided a wealth of historical information for later generations. By the time the first board minutes were recorded in October 1868, there had apparently already been a decision made to advertise for courthouse site locations. On November 6, 1868, two bids were received and opened: one from Nancy Parshley (widow of John Parshley) for the location where the current Suwannee County Courthouse is located, and the other from Nathan H. Walker and Henry A. Wyse (also spelled "Wise") where Azalea Court is now located (adjacent to the street named for Nathan Walker). Walker had been a business partner of John Parshley, and Wyse was a prominent businessman. After reviewing the bids, the county commissioners decided to accept the Parshley proposal.

However, at the next board meeting on December 8, 1868, the Parshley proposal was withdrawn by her agent/son-in-law, John Brock. Nathan Walker and Henry Wyse immediately proposed the construction of a courthouse on the previously submitted lot adjoining the current Walker Street. They added that the courthouse would be finished by the following May. The Suwannee County Board of County Commissioners accepted this proposal at the same December meeting, and Walker and Wyse began construction of the new courthouse.

Unfortunately for Wyse and Walker, by the regular board meeting in February 1869, it was determined that one of the county commissioners at the December meeting was not qualified to serve and had been subsequently removed from office. As a result, there had not been a qualified quorum at the meeting in December 1868, and the actions of that meeting (including the rescinding of the Parshley courthouse proposal and acceptance of the Walker courthouse proposal) were declared null and void. In the meantime, the Florida legislature had changed the laws to allow citizens to decide on the location of their county seat in January 1869 (apparently based on numerous complaints by Suwannee County citizens who wished to decide where their own county seat would be located). The county commissioners therefore ordered an election held to allow the citizens to choose the location of the county seat.

An election was held on March 27, 1869, after being advertised for four weeks in the *Live Oak Advertiser* (the local newspaper). There was some discussion among the commissioners, but it appeared that they decided to vote upon one of three sites for the county seat: the Parshley site, the Walker site and the old courthouse site in Houston. There were six polling places for this first election: Houston, Wellborn, Live Oak, Columbus, Plowdens and (New) Boston. The results were inconclusive; Houston received 215 votes, the Parshley site in Live Oak received 168 and there were 91 votes for Live Oak. There were major problems with the voting, such as votes by deceased citizens and people voting twice. The county commissioners were unsure of how many sites were actually being voted on!

Due to the various problems, the first vote was thrown out, and a new vote was demanded and duly advertised in the *Live Oak Advertiser*. The commissioners decided that only two sites would be in the running this time: the Parshley site in Live Oak and the old courthouse in Houston. This second vote on May 15 resulted in a comfortable majority of voters selecting the Parshley site over Houston, and Nancy Parshley submitted a deed to be recorded in the clerk's office for the lot on which a courthouse would be built. Until a building was constructed, the Suwannee County commissioners rented the Baptist church in Live Oak (originally built by John Parshley) at a cost of one dollar for each board meeting and two dollars a day for each circuit court hearing. But what about the nearly complete building that Walker and Wyse had been constructing?

Due to the changes in the law and the recent election, Nathan Walker and Henry Wyse now had a nearly complete building that was no longer designated the county courthouse. Worse yet, its construction had not been compensated by the county commissioners. This lack of payment brought Walker, the owner of the property, some financial difficulty. In order to salvage his investment, Nathan Walker quickly gathered a host of local businessmen and Nancy Parshley, widow of former business associate John Parshley, to find a use for the building. On September 7, the group met and formed the Suwannee School Company, a private corporation that would compete with the newly created Suwannee County Board of Public Instruction (more commonly known as the Suwannee County School Board) to educate the youth of the area. This private company would use Walker and Wyse's proposed courthouse as a school known as the Live Oak White Male and Female Seminary ("White" is underlined in the original Articles of Incorporation). The original directors of the school were Cyprian Brinson, R.L. Wiggins, John Rice, John Irvine, John Brock, George White, Joseph Sherwood, Elijah Henderson and Daniel Tedder, all prominent businessmen and/or politicians in the area.

Meanwhile, the county commissioners were working to provide a courthouse to the community. In August 1869, they bought the Baptist church originally constructed by John Parshley for $300 through Clerk of Court Nelson Conner, who was apparently acting on behalf of the First Baptist Church. Conner, besides serving as clerk of court, was also a businessman, hotel owner and preacher. He moved the church to the Parshley lot, where the current courthouse now stands.

However, not everyone associated with the Baptist church was happy with this turn of events. A report submitted to the county commissioners by the First Baptist Church Committee and still in existence at the clerk's office states that the Baptist Church Committee was "credibly informed that the said building, prior to its being sold by Mr. Conner, to said commissioners, was desecrated by being used as a place of assembling boisterous political meetings, also that it has been used as an election precinct." According to the same document, Nelson Conner had sold the church building to the county without having consulted the church trustees. Deed Book B of the county's records shows that a deed authorizing Nelson Conner to act as official agent for the Baptist Church was recorded in the second half of 1869, with supposed signatures by W.F. Bynum, Council Ward, J.O. Carroll, T.R. Compton, Nancy M. Parshley, John H. Baker and Nelson Conner. The writing, as with the recorded copy of every other document from the time, is in the handwriting of the clerk (there was no photocopying ability then). Oddly enough, however, there is no third-party authentication of the signatures, as is found on other recorded documents. It is quite possible that Nelson Conner, seeing an opportunity for profit, forged the document and signatures, as he would be the one to record it in the deed book anyway.

Whatever the true nature of the sale of the Baptist church building, it was used for only a short time as the Suwannee County Courthouse before it was destroyed just before the commissioners' meeting of May 13, 1870. Board minutes state that the loss was because Nelson Conner, "having failed to put said House in its proper place, and being left in an insecure condition, has been blown down." The next month, Conner formally protested that the commissioners had not paid him the $300 due for the church building purchase (despite its subsequent loss), but the commissioners postponed the decision for a later meeting. The board of county commissioners, again without a courthouse, held meetings upstairs above the nearby Parshley Store, free of charge for the first year.

John Parshley had built the Parshley Store presumably just after moving to Live Oak around 1866. His wife, Nancy, and their children even lived there briefly when they moved down to Live Oak the next year while their two-story home was being constructed across from the present courthouse. The Parshley Store itself was located on the northwest corner of Howard Street and Ohio Avenue. Dr. H.F. Airth purchased the lot from the heirs of Nancy Parshley in April 1898 and then sold it to C.Y. Byrd in July. By the end of the year, Byrd had constructed a brick building on the location, and it still stands today.

Meanwhile, Conner was in dire financial straits because of the refusal of the board to pay him for the Baptist church. He turned to Nancy Parshley to call in an old favor. Apparently, before his death in August 1868, John Parshley had sold three lots in Live Oak to Conner. The contract stipulated that Parshley would wipe away Conner's debt for the three properties if Conner could have the county seat moved to Live Oak and then build, with Conner's own money, a courthouse on the Parshley lot (which was across the street from Parshley's home). Although the county seat moved to Live Oak, Conner had not built a courthouse using his own funds. He went to Nancy Parshley in 1870 to ask for the satisfactions of mortgage for the three downtown properties he had received from John Parshley, despite the fact that he had not yet paid for them. Nancy Parshley, a shrewd businesswoman in her own right, refused to hand them over because Conner had not abided by the terms of the agreement. Conner then informed Mrs. Parshley that he would simply go to the newspapers with the fact that the Parshleys had been involved in negotiations to have the county seat moved and then officially record the contract between Parshley and Conner for all the world to see. Mrs. Parshley, in tears, agreed to give Conner the satisfactions of mortgage for the three lots, thus writing off some $2,200 (more than $40,000 today) that Conner had not yet paid.

Nancy Parshley, not to be duped, then sued Conner for blackmail. Since Nelson Conner was the clerk of court, he was in the predicament of receiving documents professionally that detailed a suit against him personally! Conner appears to have carried out his clerk's duties faithfully, since the original documents of the lawsuit still exist in the records of the clerk's office. However, Conner's political position did not help him; later in the year, he lost the case. As a result of losing the lawsuit, Conner's family had to sell off several properties and belongings to pay off Parshley. Nelson Conner died in February 1871; it is possible that the lawsuit, subsequent financial loss and humiliation had something to do with his death. The leaders of the Baptist Church sued the board of county commissioners for the loss of their illegally obtained building in a lawsuit that would drag on until July 5, 1886, when both parties finally consented to drop the matter. Meanwhile, the courthouse drama was still unfolding.

The county commissioners had been meeting above the Parshley Store since the 1870 loss of the Baptist church building that had served briefly as the Suwannee County Courthouse. In 1871, the commissioners decided that they needed a proper courthouse and therefore advertised for bids. However, the bids did not include a stipulation requiring construction of a building on the Parshley lot as had been decided by the voters less than two years before. This failure led to feuding between the board of county commissioners and local businessmen.

One of the proposals for a new courthouse (whose paperwork still survives in the clerk's office) was submitted by Elijah Franklin Henderson. It called for his Live Oak White Male and Female Seminary to be adequately renovated to accommodate the various functions of the county. The seminary building was none other than Nathan Walker's proposed courthouse from two years earlier! Walker had been one of the Suwannee School Company's original incorporators in 1869 (after the failure to move the county seat to his site) and allowed the school company to use his building. Soon thereafter, Walker's business ventures failed and he went into great debt, including $4,000 that he owed Nancy Parshley for his portion of the sawmill and lumberyard that Walker had jointly owned with John Parshley. Unable to pay his debts, Walker fled "out west" to Chicago on the night of October 31/November 1, 1871, never to return. Among the land and structures foreclosed upon or sold by Nathan Walker was his proposed courthouse, which had become the Live Oak White Male and Female Seminary, which Elijah Henderson had purchased. Henderson saw an opportunity and thus submitted his proposal to the Suwannee County Board of County Commissioners in 1871. Reviewing the bids, the county commissioners selected the Henderson proposal as the county's new courthouse. At last, the building originally constructed by Nathan Walker and Henry Wyse as a courthouse would serve in that role. Or so it was thought.

John S. Purviance was a longtime citizen and businessman whose store was located near the Parshley site, which voters had determined two years before would be the county site. As a result of the board's decision to use the Henderson building as the courthouse, Purviance filed a lawsuit on behalf of all those who stood to lose business from a relocated courthouse. The lawsuit included the fact that "the present Board of County Commissioners in utter disregard of the wishes of a majority of the voters in locating the County cite [*sic*] according to law, are now contracting for the erection of a Court House on a lot near half a mile from the area designated by the voters of the County, as two years have not elapsed since said election." State law at the time deemed that once the voters determined a location for the county site, it could not be moved for ten years (if in a wooden building) or twenty years (if in a brick building); this would allow some normalcy of operations and stop yearly changes to where people had to go to perform government functions.

The Purviance lawsuit continued for many months until Judge William Bryson ordered the county commissioners to construct a courthouse on the Parshley lot and pay all court costs related to Purviance's lawsuit. In 1872, before the lawsuit was complete, John S. Purviance became a Suwannee County commissioner, finding himself in the unusual predicament of suing himself: John Purviance the citizen suing the members of the board of county commissioners, which now included John Purviance the commissioner! The issue seemed to quickly resolve itself when a committee was formed in the same year (with Purviance being one of its members) to look into erecting a courthouse on the Parshley lot.

In July 1873, after receiving several bids from around north Florida, a contract was signed with Willis Ball of Leon County to build a two-story, 5,400-square-foot wood courthouse at a price of $8,000 (over $150,000 today) on the land donated by Nancy Parshley. The existing agreement and specifications show that the courthouse was 60 feet by 45 feet in size with 12-foot ceilings and was made of the finest yellow pine and painted with two coats of white paint. Letters still in the custody of the clerk of court's office record some of the negotiations between Ball and the board of county commissioners. Ball even left for posterity the reason that he had been delayed in coming to Live Oak to begin work on the courthouse: he had a bout of diarrhea that lasted one month!

Despite his temporary illness (which may have been related to his death a year or two later), Willis Ball carried out his construction duties faithfully. County commission minutes from September 8, 1873, show that Ball used local businessman John Frasier for some of the materials. Board minutes of March 2, 1874, record the division of the first floor of the almost-complete

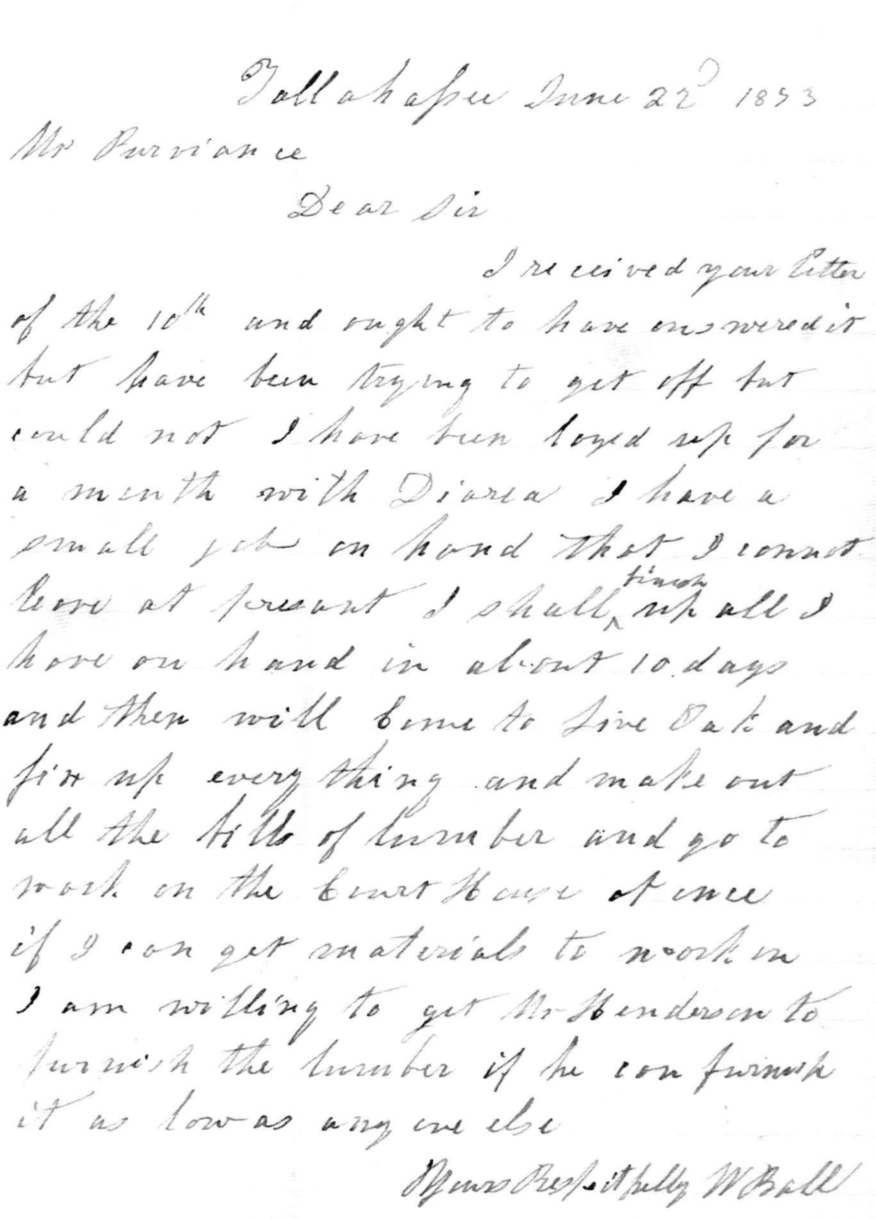

Tallahassee June 22d 1873
Mr Purviance
Dear Sir
I received your Letter of the 10th and ought to have answered it but have been trying to get off but could not I have been layed up for a month with Diarea I have a small job on hand that I cannot leave at present I shall finish up all I have on hand in about 10 days and then will come to Live Oak and fix up every thing and make out all the bills of lumber and go to work on the Court House at once if I can get materials to work on I am willing to get Mr Henderson to furnish the lumber if he can furnish it as low as any one else
Yours Respectfully W Ball

Letter from Willis Ball to the Suwannee County Board of County Commissioners regarding courthouse construction delay, June 22, 1873. *Suwannee County Clerk of Court.*

courthouse among the various constitutional officers. The clerk of the court would occupy the northeast room, the judge of county court would occupy the southeast room, the sheriff and tax collector would occupy the southwest room and the county treasurer (an elected position abolished in 1917) would occupy the northwest room. The second floor was where court and board meetings would be held.

On March 23, the board of county commissioners authorized a contract for the painting of the courthouse and construction of suitable furniture, to be completed by the next regular meeting. On April 6, 1874, the board accepted the new courthouse from Willis Ball and authorized chairman John S. Purviance to insure the building on the best terms possible. This was completed by the next meeting on April 25, as on that date, the board authorized ninety dollars to pay the insurance premiums of the Franklin Fire Insurance Company of Philadelphia and the Virginia Fire and Marine Insurance Company of Richmond to cover the new courthouse. By the end of 1874, county government had settled into the newly completed wood courthouse constructed by Willis Ball.

With a new courthouse finally under construction in Live Oak at the Parshley site, what happened to the courthouse and lot in Houston that had served as the county seat for nearly ten years? At its September 8, 1873 meeting, the board of county commissioners authorized County Treasurer Matthias M. Blackburn to sell them from the front door of the courthouse in Live Oak to the highest bidder. The highest bid at the November 12, 1873 auction was only twenty-five dollars. The county treasurer then petitioned the board of county commissioners to allow him to seek alternative means for getting rid of the property. On November 13, the board rescinded its authorization for Blackburn to sell the old courthouse at public auction and instead authorized him to sell the property at a private sale, subject to the board's approval. Nothing further was done on this for some time, but it is interesting to note that at its May 5, 1874 meeting, the Suwannee Board of County Commissioners ordered County Treasurer Blackburn to discontinue the selling of any lands belonging to the county after that date. The old courthouse apparently sat unused for several more years, although it might have been a polling place for local elections in the Houston District.

Eventually, on April 7, 1877, the county commissioners ordered that the old courthouse at Houston be given to Thomas T. Hurst. This made sense, as Hurst had been the original owner of the forty acres on which the courthouse stood and had already received from the board the remaining unsold portions in 1869 (after Houston was no longer the county seat). However, the specific deed giving the old courthouse to Hurst was not recorded in the deed books of the clerk of court. The recording of deeds during this period was haphazard at best, with some deeds not being recorded for decades after the sale. Furthermore, deed records of the time were very subjective; instead of objective locations like "Lot 3 of Block A of so-and-so subdivision," they were more like, "bounded on the north by lands of John Smith, east by a road, south by a lot formerly owned by John Doe, and on the west by an alley." Even worse are the deeds with legal descriptions of "so many feet west of the big oak tree" or "along the line of three turkey oak trees."

After much research, the author's estimated guess is that the building was located on "Main Street" (the Live Oak and Houston Road, now U.S. 90), possibly in Blocks 9, 14 or 15 of the old plat of Houston. For reference, Block 9 is the current location of the Union Baptist Church that was deeded to the African American community by Thomas Hurst in 1886. At any event, the original building appears to be long gone. The author has yet to find any confirmed photographs or information describing Suwannee County's first purpose-built courthouse.

By 1904, the drastic increase in Suwannee County's population had necessitated a larger courthouse. The county commissioners advertised for

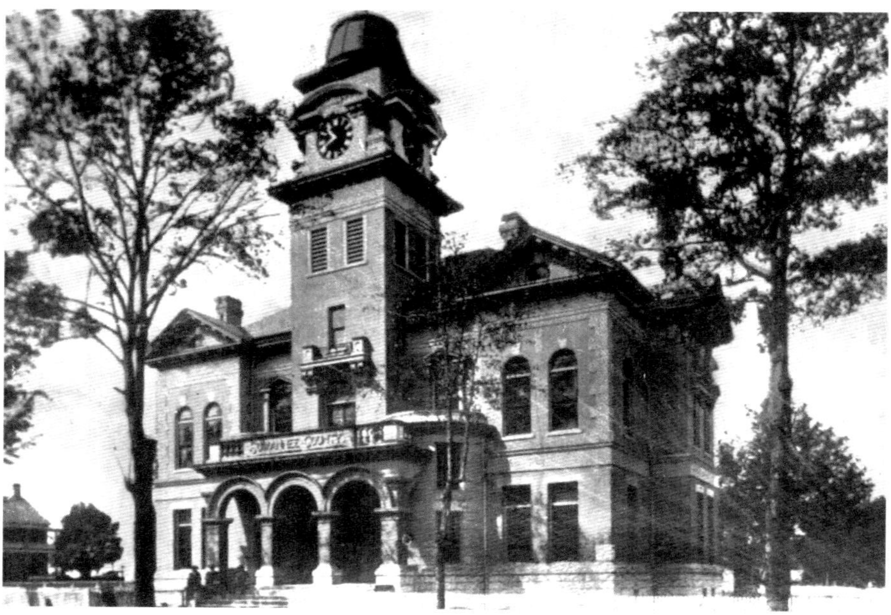

Suwannee County Courthouse, early 1900s. *Suwannee County Historical Museum.*

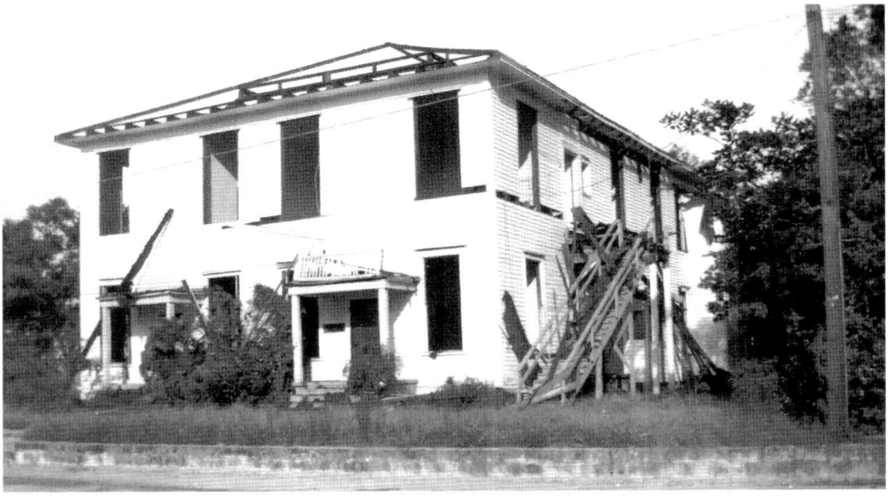

Old Suwannee County Courthouse, probably during demolition, circa 1970. The caption on the back of the photograph reads that it was "under repair." *Suwannee County Clerk of Court.*

bids, and a larger, brick courthouse was completed by the end of 1904. That courthouse still serves today as the center of government functions, one of the oldest in Florida still being used for its original purpose.

Before the construction of the current brick courthouse could begin in 1904, the old wood courthouse built in 1873–74 was moved to the corner of Pine Avenue and Wilbur Street to make way for the new one. There it operated as a boardinghouse under the names of the "Brown House" and the "White House" for many years. In or just prior to 1947, the wood courthouse was moved a few hundred feet south on Pine Avenue by Fred J. Green to make way for a new concrete building (since replaced by the county jail). The twice-moved former courthouse was then used as apartments for another twenty-odd years. By the late 1960s, however, time had taken its toll, and the old courthouse was torn down approximately one hundred years after its completion. Its location eventually became the southernmost portion of the county jail and the driveway leading from the post office parking lot to Pine Avenue.

# 3

# JACK-OF-ALL-TRADES

## *Gus Potsdamer*

Some events and characters in history will make you smile, laugh or drop your jaw in disbelief. One such character is Gottshalk Augustus "Gus" Potsdamer. In fact, Gus Potsdamer is probably one of the most interesting characters you'll ever read about in Suwannee County's history.

Potsdamer, of German descent, was born in 1853, according to his tombstone. He grew up as a Jew during a time of general anti-Semitism around the world. By the 1870s, Potsdamer lived in Lake City. According to the July 11, 1876 *Savannah Morning News*, on July 3, 1876, Gus and a friend, George Harris, narrowly escaped death on one of the lakes around Lake City. Their rowboat capsized; if it had not been for nearby assistance, they would certainly have drowned. Gus was liked in the Lake City community, enough to be elected town marshal (now called chief of police) prior to 1880.

By late January 1880, Town Marshal Potsdamer had a long-running heated dispute with the Columbia County sheriff, John C. Henry. The conflict escalated into a fistfight when the two met on Main Street (now Marion Street), and Potsdamer fatally wounded Henry with a pistol. According to the February 3, 1880 edition of the *Savannah Morning News*, the men had met in a saloon after seeing a performance of the Park Theatre Troupe. A personal quarrel began that spilled into the streets. The newspaper described the fight and mortal wounding of Henry, lamenting the fact that "they are both young men of reputation and promise, though both of rather rash and hasty tempers, and the unfortunate difficulty between them is regretted by the whole community."

Gus Potsdamer was charged and tried for first-degree murder, convicted of second-degree murder and sentenced to life in prison at the state convict camp near Live Oak. The jury's recommendation of mercy saved him from hanging. Potsdamer's conviction was controversial, with many reports stating that Sheriff Henry had started the trouble and was beating Potsdamer over the head with the butt of his pistol when Potsdamer got loose and killed him. Furthermore, Potsdamer was very popular and had a reputation as a city marshal who always enforced the law fairly.

Because he was Jewish, and because he had killed a lawman, it was feared that Potsdamer would be lynched by one faction or rescued by another. J.C. Powell, captain of the state's convict camp in Suwannee County, wrote about taking custody of Potsdamer in his book *American Siberia*:

> *When the train from Lake City pulled in, a large crowd had assembled at the depot, and five men with shotguns first disembarked. Then came the prisoner, a frail, pallid young man, so loaded down with chains, handcuffs, shackles, and manacles of every description that he could hardly walk, and another guard of five men brought up the rear. Almost all of the prominent Hebrews of the state came pouring out of the cars after this procession.*

The new Columbia County sheriff and state attorney asked Powell where the posse was that would escort Potsdamer to the convict camp. Powell replied that he alone would take Potsdamer to the camp and unchained him for the four-mile walk. Potsdamer was thankful for the kindness that Powell showed him, and the book reported that Powell made "staunch friends" of the Jewish people that day. Potsdamer served only thirty days in the convict camp before he was released while his case was on appeal.

The July 21, 1880 *Savannah Morning News* quoted the *Live Oak Bulletin*:

> *On last Monday night, Mr. Gus Potsdamer was returned to the convict camps by order of the Supreme Court, which sustained the action of the court below, and refused to grant a new trial in his case. It will be remembered that at the last fall term of the Circuit Court for Columbia County, Mr. Potsdamer, who had been indicted for the killing of Sheriff John Henry, was convicted of murder in the second degree, and sentenced to the penitentiary for ninety-nine years. His attorneys asked for a new trial, which was refused by Judge Cocke, who was then presiding, and an appeal was taken to the Supreme Court, with the result as above stated. Mr.*

> *Potsdamer has many strong friends and sympathizers, and we presume that a mighty effort will be made to secure a pardon for him.*

Potsdamer's friends did in fact appeal his murder conviction through the legal system and eventually won the case. Gus Potsdamer was released after only two months of incarceration. According to Captain J.C. Powell of the convict camp in Live Oak, Potsdamer took his incarceration good-naturedly. Afterward, Potsdamer would speak often of Powell as his "old boss."

By 1884, Potsdamer had moved to Live Oak and become a respected businessman in several ventures. On April 9, 1884, he was elected to the Live Oak Town Council, a position he served in until resigning on February 15, 1886. From minutes of the period, it seems that many men who served in various local government capacities resigned before their terms were up. The May 23, 1884 issue of the *Lake City Reporter* noted that the progressive Potsdamer had inaugurated a movement to "telephone" Live Oak—in other words, to provide telephone service using Alexander Graham Bell's practical telephone patented less than ten years before. The same newspaper issue notes that Potsdamer ran a fine livery stable, a billiard and poolroom and the "Pastime," which was noted for "refreshments for the inner system of mankind." An ad in the same paper reads, "O, ye denizens of dry towns, lend an ear and order your 'little brown jugs'—the best in the land—from Gus Potsdamer, Live Oak, Fla. Prompt attention given to orders."

Gus Potsdamer is also mentioned in the May 23, 1885 edition of the *Tropical Paradise*, a newspaper from Jacksonville, as having a turnout service (a taxi service using a horse and buggy) that traveled between Live Oak and the health resorts in nearby White Springs. The November 14, 1885 edition of the *Florida Bulletin* (a predecessor to the *Suwannee Democrat*) mentions Potsdamer's many endeavors. Besides his businesses at the time, he ran a livery and stable and sold carriages, harnesses, liquor and buggies (including the popular T.T. Haydock variety). He also served on the Live Oak Town Council. The same year, Gus Potsdamer was first lieutenant of the Suwannee Guards (the local militia unit that was later known as the Suwannee Rifles). The unit was under the command of Captain A.L. Woodward; William Bryson was the second lieutenant. The Suwannee Guards had five sergeants and corporals, as well as forty-six privates in its fifty-eight-man total.

On February 7, 1887, Gus Potsdamer was appointed "Scavenger for the town of Live Oak" by the town council; the closest modern-day equivalent of this would be the sanitation department director. The official duties of such a "scavenger" would be to collect all ashes, waste and garbage around town and dispose of it. Potsdamer probably did not remain in this position long; he was sworn in as duly elected town marshal and tax collector on April 26 of the same year. Potsdamer was now fulfilling a similar role in Live Oak to the one he had in Lake City less than ten years prior. This time, however, there were no lethal fights with the sheriff! At the time, the town and the county had their own tax collectors, a position now handled by the Suwannee County tax collector. Potsdamer served in that capacity for less than three months; on July 5, he resigned from the positions of town marshal and tax collector. This was not the end of his political career, however.

On October 21, 1889, the town council voted to go to Potsdamer to secure the use of a hall for meetings. The most likely explanation was that, because Suwannee County became a dry county in 1889, Gus had to close his liquor establishment and thus had the space available. Either way, the transaction was approved, because multiple town council minutes discuss the payment of rent to Gus Potsdamer until April 3, 1894, when the new Masonic lodge was approved for use by the council.

Potsdamer continued to be well liked by the community. He had enough support to be elected Suwannee County sheriff in 1889, in which capacity he served until 1893. During his time as sheriff, he became known for hunting down fugitives of the law and otherwise keeping order in the county.

According to the *Waycross Reporter* of December 21, 1889, Potsdamer arrested a man named Robert McCoy for carrying concealed weapons. McCoy told Potsdamer, "You have arrested me for something else than carrying a gun, and can't fool me in this way."

"What else?" asked Potsdamer, and McCoy admitted to a murder that he had committed a few weeks before. McCoy also gave the names of the others involved in the murder. Potsdamer and others had been looking for the unknown murderers for weeks without luck, and then one admitted to the killing when arrested for a relatively minor infraction! Potsdamer turned McCoy and his information over to the proper authorities; McCoy and the others were either hanged for their crime or killed while attempting to evade capture.

Sheriff Potsdamer's enforcement of the law continued. The July 8, 1890 edition of the *Indianapolis Journal* states, "A notorious negro outlaw, supposed to be Bob Brewer, the Jessup murderer, who also shot a deputy sheriff at Boardman, last week, was captured near Live Oak, Fla, Sunday night, by Sheriff Potsdamer."

Unfortunately, others would sometimes trump Potsdamer's official duties. On December 18, 1891, a mob of dozens of masked men (about one hundred men, according to the *Sacramento Daily Union*, and about thirty men according to a Fulton County, Georgia newspaper) jumped off a train passing through Live Oak and made their way to the residence of Sheriff Potsdamer. Armed with rifles and revolvers, they seized the outgunned and outnumbered Potsdamer and took from him the keys to the county jail. Rushing to the jail behind the courthouse, the mob then took from a cell two African American men suspected of the murder of H.D. Parramore of Valdosta on the streets of New Branford (now Branford) the week before. The mob hanged the two men from a tree a short distance from the jail and riddled the bodies with bullets before fleeing the scene.

In addition to his government positions, Gus Potsdamer also continued to run several businesses in the late 1800s and early 1900s. In 1889, he expanded his livery and stable business by purchasing the livery and stable of the deceased W.F. Bynum Jr. that was situated on the southwest corner of Duval Street and Ohio Avenue; this site later became the location of the Masonic lodge. In 1892, Potsdamer purchased the building on Conner Street in which he had been running his original livery and stable business for several years as he continued his expansion. He was also an undertaker and ran other businesses, many of which sold alcohol (at least when Suwannee was a wet county). In 1892, Potsdamer purchased Live Oak's artesian well from C.H. and Mamie Tedder for $200. This well, used for many years to provide Live Oak with drinking water, was located approximately where the Live Oak Fire Department stands today on Duval Street. He sold the property to Thomas Dowling in 1897, the same time that he sold additional property to Dowling a block farther east to be used as the location for the Dowling Waterworks (later the City of Live Oak's waterworks).

Despite being a lawman off and on for many years, Potsdamer did not always follow the law. While sheriff in 1888, he was sued by John M. Lawrence for payment of wages. It seems that the former sheriff had received a request to pay wages, and Potsdamer refused to comply after he entered office. Potsdamer was found guilty and sentenced to pay not only the past wages but also the court costs. In 1891, William Adams filed a lawsuit against Potsdamer for false imprisonment and extortion. According to Adams, Potsdamer had falsely imprisoned him for six hours and then extorted $10 from him to secure his release. Adams sued for $5,000 in damages.

Beyond lawsuits brought against him as sheriff, Gus Potsdamer had several other run-ins with the law. Suwannee County court records have several instances of him being charged with things like "holding shop without a license" and "selling liquor without a license." In September 1897, for instance, he was found guilty of possessing 150 bottles of liquor and 150 bottles of beer in violation of the 1889 election that had made the county dry. Earlier in the year, he had been charged (along with several other individuals) with selling whiskey, brandy, wine, rum, gin and malt beer. He posted a $500 bond, and the trial began in May 1897. He pled guilty, and his sentence was suspended upon payment of costs. Similar charges from the same period were continued until the next court term for years before apparently being dropped.

Potsdamer was actually convicted on December 19, 1895, of "engaging in business of a retail liquor dealer without paying the special tax" in Jacksonville. His sentence was thirty days in the Duval County Jail and a fine of $100. He received a presidential pardon for this charge on May 28, 1897 (he must have had friends in high places!). Gus was charged in 1899 in Suwannee County for cohabitating with Sallie Reese without being married to her. He paid his $250 bail; in December 1902, a jury found them not guilty. Potsdamer always seemed to get out of serious trouble, and apparently it did not impact his political ambitions.

Potsdamer became the first fire chief when the Live Oak Fire Department was established on September 30, 1903, with a budget of $1,240. It was housed in a small shed on the northeast corner of the courthouse yard (this was before there was a dedicated city hall) and comprised two hose carts, sixty feet of fire hose and two firefighters, along with sixteen volunteers. Potsdamer served as fire chief until he resigned in June 1906. He was replaced by H.H. Hair, one of his original firefighters. Potsdamer continued running his other businesses during this time. In 1907, he is listed as a merchant in Live Oak with a stock of less than $1,000. An article in the April 23, 1907 *Live Oak Daily Democrat* states, "Potsdamer & Bird is a new firm here to supply Florida stall-fed beef to butchers in this section." In addition, a number of obituaries and articles comment on Potsdamer's coffins and his undertaker business in Live Oak.

After nearly a quarter century out of office, Potsdamer again ran for sheriff of Suwannee County in the 1912 election. One of his campaign ads (from either 1911 or early 1912) states, among other things:

> *If you elect me to fill the office of Sheriff, I promise to be faithful to the obligation of that office and live up to the oath that I will take when I enter upon the duties prescribed by law. I shall employ only competent deputies, and shall personally do those things the Sheriff should attend to. I shall personally look after the court house, yard, and jail, and see that they are*

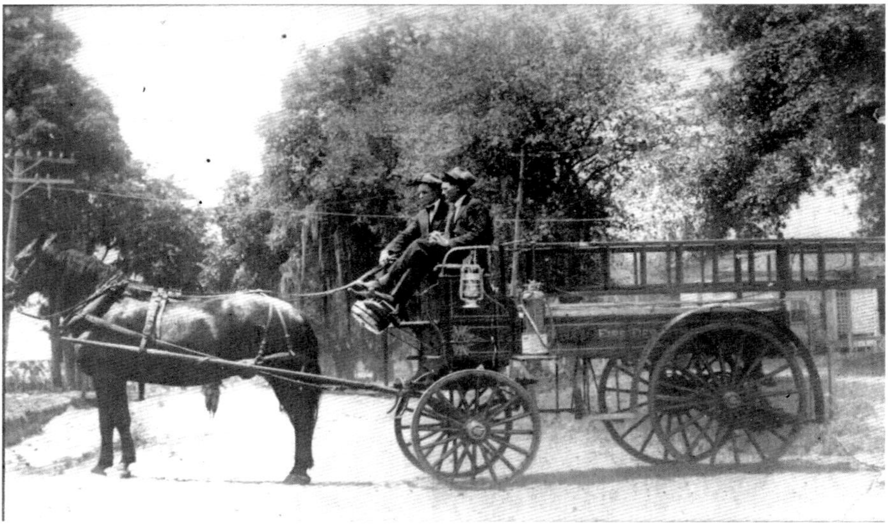

Old Lee the horse with members of the Live Oak Fire Department in the early 1900s. *City of Live Oak.*

> *kept clean, and that the prisoners have plenty of good wholesome food, such as the law permits; and during my entire term will strictly attend to the Sheriff's office, if you elect me.*

Potsdamer's ads seemed to pay off—he was elected sheriff near the end of 1912, taking office on January 7, 1913. However, his enforcement of the law was somewhat lax this time around. This could have been because of his continued undertaking business. The *Suwannee Democrat*, as quoted in volume 51 of the *Inland Printer* of 1913, stated:

> *At the solicitation of old friends, Sheriff Potsdamer has consented to continue in the undertaking business, as he can do so without in the least interfering with his duties as sheriff. Mr. Potsdamer has been interested in the undertaking business in this city for years, and his old friends would not hear to his giving up the business.*

One of the first duties of Sheriff Potsdamer was to repair the jail and then remove the fence surrounding the courthouse yard. The pickets from the fence would then be sold to the highest bidder for cash, according to the January 7, 1913 minutes of the Suwannee County Board of County

Commissioners. As requested by locals, Potsdamer continued his undertaking business throughout his second tenure as sheriff. There are several instances in the board of county commissioners' minutes where he was paid for coffins and for performing burials (probably for paupers). Potsdamer also provided rewards for the capture of certain criminals, but the board did not always unanimously go along with this. The June 4, 1914 minutes state that Sheriff Potsdamer had paid $50 (about $1,200 today) for the capture of Allen Fort and that two commissioners refused to pay it.

On September 2, 1913, the Suwannee County Board of County Commissioners authorized $300 (approximately $7,000 in today's money) to Sheriff Potsdamer for the purchase of two bloodhounds to pursue criminals. However, the sheriff apparently pocketed the money or otherwise squandered it. The commissioners made an attempt in October 1914 to have the money returned via an official resolution, but if it was done, it was not recorded in the board's minutes. This action, coupled with his general lack of law enforcement (especially when it concerned illegal alcohol sales), led to Potsdamer being suspended from the office of sheriff by Governor Park Trammell on December 22, 1914, effective December 31.

Among the governor's stated reasons for removing Potsdamer was that, during his present term, the sheriff had

> *failed to use reasonable and proper diligence and efforts to detect and bring before the courts parties selling intoxicating liquors within the said county in violation of the law; and it being shown by the evidence before me that during the present term of office of said Sheriff violations of the law prohibiting the sale of liquors have been flagrant within said county; and it further appearing from the Auditor's report that while the said Potsdamer, upon the date that the report was made, had accounted for and paid all the fines collected by him, that he had been dilatory and slow in paying over the fines collected by him, having delayed payment in some instances for several months, and having quite generally failed to pay over the fines collected by him within the time required by law; and it appearing that the conduct above referred to of the said Potsdamer as such Sheriff constitutes neglect of duty in office.*

The Florida Senate studied the governor's suspension and, on May 14, 1915, agreed with his findings. As a result, the senate consented to the removal of Gus Potsdamer from the office of sheriff effective immediately. He was replaced by W.H. Lyle, who had been appointed acting sheriff

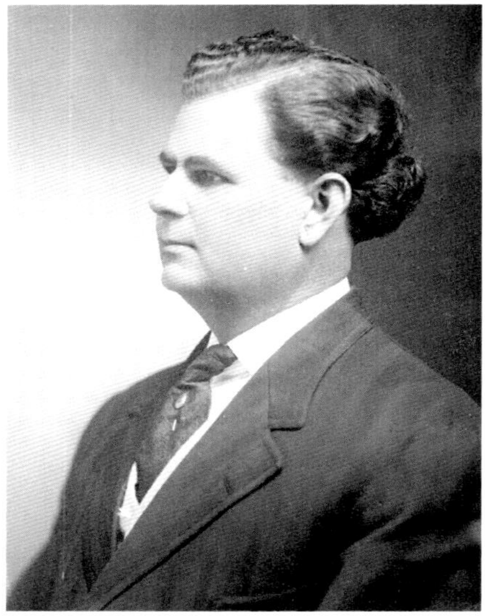

*Right*: Governor Park Trammell, who removed Sheriff Gus Potsdamer from office, circa 1915. *State Archives of Florida*.

*Below*: Tombstone of Gus Potsdamer in Jacksonville, Florida, circa 2000. *FindAGrave.com*.

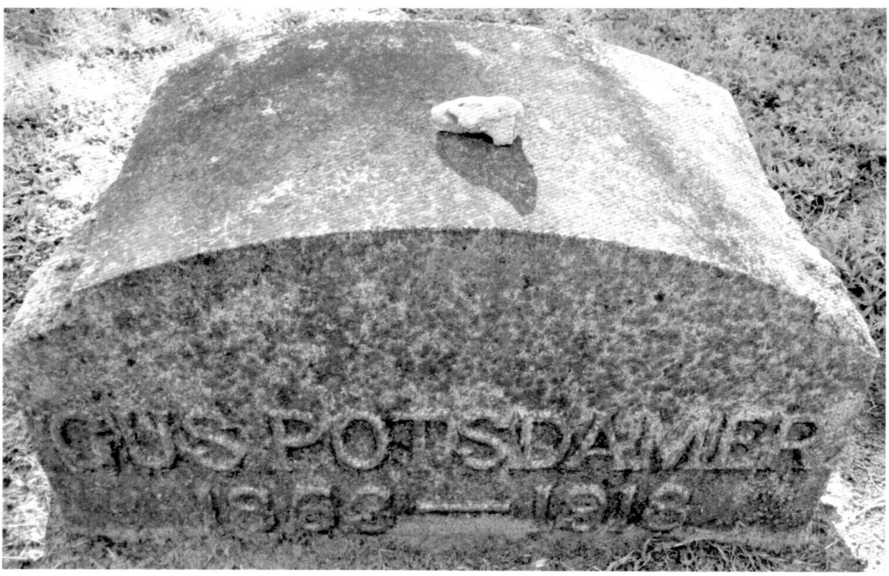


during Potsdamer's suspension and who would remain sheriff until his death in 1934.

Despite the apparent shame in being removed from office, Potsdamer remained in Live Oak, at least for a time. He appears to have enjoyed other pursuits, including sports. In the early years of the twentieth century, Live Oak had a reputation for good sports teams, especially baseball, and

Potsdamer appears to have been one of their staunch supporters. According to the July 23, 1915 edition of the *Palatka News*, Live Oak's baseball team "was regarded as the finest aggregation of semi-professional ball tossers in Florida." Unfortunately, the team lost to Palatka in a series of games that week, even after having hired experienced professional players from Charleston, South Carolina, and the Georgia State League after the first day of defeats to serve as ringers. After the defeats, the *Palatka News* reported, "Thursday was another wet day, especially for Live Oak, where it is said that old Gottschalk Pottsdammer [*sic*], as he read the telegraph bulletins from Palatka, wept a continuous stream of tears and refused to be comforted." He really got into his baseball!

By all accounts, Gus Potsdamer lived a very interesting life. The January 5, 1918 *Jacksonville Times* states,

> *Gus Pottsdammer* [sic], *63, a well known resident of Live Oak, died in this city early yesterday morning, after an illness of over a year's duration. He was formerly sheriff of Suwannee County and for many years was engaged in the undertaking business at Live Oak. The funeral took place yesterday afternoon, Rabbi I.L. Kaplan, of the Temple Ahavath Chesed officiating. The interment was in Temple cemetery.*

Few Suwannee County individuals could claim to have led the varied and charmed life that Gus Potsdamer lived!

4

# MAN'S BEST FRIEND

## *Beulah the Dog*

It is said that a dog is man's best friend. One may never know, but within the annals of Suwannee County's history was a dog that could lend credence to that old saying.

Hugh Lewis was sheriff of Suwannee County from 1953 until he died in office in 1963. Before his tenure as sheriff, Lewis had served as a superintendent of a State Road Department prison camp. In that capacity, he had trained a number of dogs to assist him in catching convicts who attempted to flee the camp.

Among Lewis's best dogs during his tenure in the prison camp was one named Jack. Jack had been able to hunt down escaped convicts on a "cold trail" many times. In 1948, Jack was put on the trail of one of the purported assailants involved in the so-called Groveland Case (a nationally known case from Lake County regarding an alleged rape and the civil rights of four African American men). The man was rumored to be in Monticello. Jack was put to work and stayed on the track for twenty-two hours until he finally caught up with the suspect. Several teams of officers rotated handling Jack throughout the long chase, switching teams when they were worn out.

A few days later, Jack was still too stiff and sore to even walk, and Hugh Lewis received another phone call to track down a criminal. He took one of his young female pups with him; she had been following simple trails from the time she was a few weeks old. By the age of six months, she was being taught how to track. Her name was Beulah. Beulah was ten months old when Hugh Lewis took her to hunt that first fugitive, and she picked up the

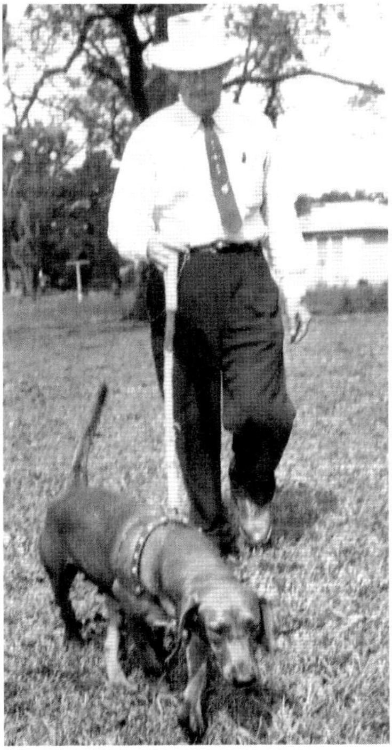

Beulah with Sheriff Hugh Lewis, circa 1950. *Wenda Lewis.*

scent like a pro. Lewis stated years later, "It was a joy to watch her work that trail during the three hours it took to catch up with the fugitive." Unfortunately for Jack, his longest chase would also be his last, as he died a short time later.

Lewis used the eighty-five-pound Beulah for every type of trail, including escaped convicts, murderers, car thieves, whiskey runners and lost children. She usually got her man (or woman, or child), but sometimes they would escape by taking a bus or car. Beulah's tracking skills became legendary; dense oak forests or swamps made no difference to her trained nose. She once trailed a moonshiner in Hamilton County into a swamp, where he had crossed into a pond and climbed a tree in the middle of it. The water was waist deep to a man and Beulah had to swim, but she swam straight to the tree with the fugitive hiding in it.

During another chase, the fugitive being tracked opened fire on Beulah and the two law enforcement officers with her. The officers were caught in the open while the fugitive fired from a dense thicket, so they dropped to the ground and returned fire on their bellies. Faithful Beulah kept low by the officers while the gunfight erupted around her. When the battle ended, she led the officers to the bushes where the now-dead fugitive lay.

The gun battle did not stop Beulah from continuing her tracking career. By the spring of 1954, Beulah had reached forty successful captures and was famous not only in Suwannee County but also around the state of Florida and the nation. Sheriff Lewis was often called upon by officers from all over north Florida to help in searches, and Beulah became a regular in the *Suwannee Democrat* as each successful capture was highlighted on the front page. Beulah's shortest chases were only two or three miles, while her longest was forty-five miles in seventeen hours through two counties. A total of fifteen officers took turns handling her leash as she hunted the two fugitives during that chase. Eventually, Beulah became so tired that she could not jump over fences and had to be lifted over, but at last she caught up with the wanted men.

In one of the many comments about Beulah in the *Suwannee Democrat*, she was reported to be back on duty after a few weeks off to wean her pups after their birth in November 1954. She kept up her tracking record, and even "dog experts" had tried to outwit Beulah, to no avail. In mid-1955, she passed sixty successful captures and kept going. When asked by a reporter if Beulah was as good as his old dog Jack, Lewis paused before saying, "I can't say that Beulah is a better dog than old Jack; maybe she is just as good, but no better."

Beulah was almost always at Sheriff Lewis's side. It didn't matter if he was driving in his car or sitting at his desk in the courthouse—Beulah was there with him. When Lewis's arthritis kept him from personally tracking fugitives with Beulah, he would send one of his sons or a deputy to track with her.

Beulah's death on September 26, 1955, was enough of a blow that it made front-page news in the next edition of the *Suwannee Democrat* and was reported in many newspapers around the United States. The *Suwannee Democrat* reported that after her last chase on September 7 (her sixty-fourth fugitive captured), in which she had traveled twenty-four miles in thirteen hours, she was found to be limping. Beulah was taken to Dr. J.D. Martin's small animal hospital, where it was discovered that she had a wooden splinter and some cactus spurs from a previous chase that had become infected. Her temperature at the time was 105 degrees (5 degrees higher than normal for a dog). Treatment began, and she seemed to be over the infection when she suffered a heart attack during her 5:30 a.m. exercise on September 26. Dr. Martin gave Beulah some adrenalin, and she appeared to respond, but two hours later she had another heart attack and died; she was a little over eight years old.

Sheriff Lewis was attending court on the morning that Beulah died, and when word was brought to him that his prized hound had passed away, he became visibly upset. Beulah "meant a lot to me; she was the best dog I ever owned," he said. In an interview with the *Sarasota Herald-Tribune*, Sheriff Lewis remarked, "It's like losing a member of the family. She was a very close friend and valued assistant." Beulah's final record of sixty-four successful captures, not including several missing children who had been found, was actually higher because no accurate counts were kept early in her career.

The *Democrat* warned fugitives and lawbreakers that they would be able to take little comfort in Beulah's passing, because her eleven-month-old son, Jack, had already been trained to take his mother's place. The day after Beulah's death, Jack occupied his mother's kennel and was ready for his first hunt. About Jack and his sibling Judy (which would also hunt criminals), Sheriff Lewis said: "They're good dogs. They've got Beulah's blood." According to the newspaper, Beulah was "taken to a quiet spot in the woods where she loved to trail so well" where she would watch her son Jack "from her seat in dogdom's Valhalla." This location was the property of her beloved master in the Sherwood Forest area of Live Oak.

Dewitt Sinclair of the Florida State Farm (who was also sheriff of Polk County between 1941 and 1949) could be rightly proud of the dog he owned that bore Beulah. Not only was Beulah famous, but several other pups from the same litter became known for their tracking abilities with law enforcement officials, including one named Fanny that worked in south Florida. Few owners could claim such fame.

# 5

# LEASING THE MOON

The Suwannee County Clerk of Court's Office is the repository of the official records of the county. Often, the information could be considered dull and monotonous, but at times, a patron will find more interesting records. Sometimes, it involves antiquated words or phrases that would be considered offensive today. Other times, the very concept of the record is enough to make one laugh.

If one were to review one of the clerk of court's random deed books (Miscellaneous Deed Book 2, to be exact), they would come across a rather fascinating entry. The deed's cover page has a picture of a large building that at first glance appears to be the U.S. Capitol. But a closer look reveals that it is actually an observatory or planetarium. The text that follows is even more interesting:

> *General Quitclaim Deed to one acre of land on the Moon (Northeast Quadrant) from the Interplanetary Development Corporation, a profit corporation dedicated to exploration of planets, public education, development of satellites, and similar activities, also rockets.*
>
> *This indenture, made the 23rd day of November, 1955, between Interplanetary Development Corporation, a domestic corporation, having its principal place of business at The Little Museum, 7 The Place, Glen Cove, Nassau County, New York, party of the first part, and (names removed for publication), party of the second part….*
>
> *All that certain plot, piece or parcel of land, situate, lying and being in the crater Copernicus, situated in the northeast quadrant of the surface of*

> *the Moon facing the planet Earth, more particularly known and described as follows: Lot No. (refer to cover of deed), comprising by admeasurement one (1) acre, more or less, as more particularly described on a certain subdivision plan, prepared and acknowledged by the grantor on 1st day of September 1955, and deposited at the office of the grantor at Glen Cove, New York, United States of America, Planet Earth....*
>
> *Together with beach rights to, and right of access to, the Sea of Tranquility for the enjoyment thereof.*
>
> *Together with the right to fish, dredge and claim in, upon and under the Sea of Nectar with the right to enter upon said Sea at the places dedicated by the Grantor for said uses and purposes.*
>
> *Together with the right to engage in Winter sports in the Lunar Alps with all the privileges appurtenant thereto without the grantor being in any manner liable for the consequences.*
>
> *Together with the privilege of prospecting for all manner of minerals and other elements in the Lunar Apennines...*

The document then ends with the usual legal statements and the signatures of the president, vice president, secretary and treasurer of the Interplanetary Development Corporation.

The 1950s was a time of great scientific discoveries and change not only in the United States but also throughout the world. The space race was being contested between the United States and the Soviet Union to determine who would make it into orbit first. The common person was fixated on the idea of space travel; many movies from the era attest to the attraction of aliens and planets. Numerous groups took advantage of this hype and began selling land not only on the Moon but also on Mars and other more distant celestial bodies.

In October 1955, Robert R. Coles, the former chairman of the Hayden Planetarium in Manhattan, incorporated the Interplanetary Development Corporation to educate the public on space and the possibilities of travel there. However, the corporation's most important work was to sell land on the Moon as if it owned it, as well as a corresponding ticket reserving a seat on the first passenger rocket there. Coles was not the first person to claim ownership of the Moon; two years before his corporation was established, a Chilean lawyer did so. In 1948, a famous American eccentric and author claimed ownership of "outer space," which would include the Moon. Others preceded him, including, supposedly, a Prussian who had been given the rights to the moon by King Frederick the Great of Prussia in 1756.

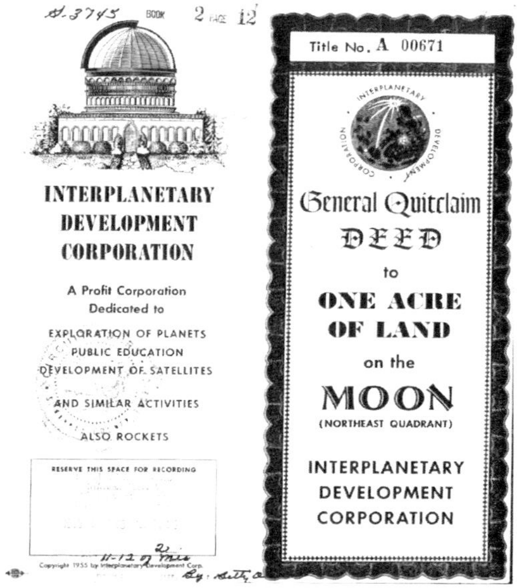


Deed from Interplanetary Development Corporation, 1955. *Suwannee County Clerk of Court.*

On being interviewed, Coles stated that he was not attempting to deceive buyers and would only offer land on the side of the Moon that faced Earth. "We wouldn't sell land we'd never seen," he said. Coles added, "We're not trying to put anything over on anybody. Anybody who's half intelligent who reads the deed will realize it's a joke," he told a reporter from *Newsday* in 1955. Some four thousand people decided to invest in the Interplanetary Development Corporation before it dissolved on September 8, 1958, eleven months after the Russians launched *Sputnik* (the first satellite in space) and eight months after the United States launched its first satellite, *Explorer I.*

When the Soviet Union landed the first unmanned satellite on the Moon (along with a Soviet flag) on September 14, 1959, the issue of who owned the Moon came to the fore. On the day of the Soviet Moon landing, the United States announced that it would reject any Soviet claim to the Moon. The Soviets denied that they were claiming ownership. The United Nations eventually sponsored the "Outer Space Treaty" in 1967 that forbade countries from claiming ownership of outer space—it was something for all of mankind to share.

Nevertheless, this brief fad with the emerging space race saw its way to Suwannee County, where a husband and wife not only purchased a Moon deed for $1 (the equivalent of about $9 in 2015 dollars) but also took the time (and spent the money) to have it recorded in the official records of Suwannee County for posterity.

# 6

# "I WAS A PILOT FLYING AN AIRPLANE"

## *Barbara Moore*

*I was a pilot flying an airplane.*
*—Francis Gary Powers*

When studying old records, one will often come across historical information that until that point had been lost to the annals of time. Sometimes, this information deals with a famous event in local, national or international history. Such is the case with some of the records held by the Suwannee County clerk of court.

Barbara Gay Moore was born on the night of November 15, 1934, at the Viola House in Live Oak (on the northwest corner of Second and Hamilton Streets, since torn down). Her twenty-eight-year-old father, Estul Moore, was a telegrapher for the Atlantic Coast Line Railroad who had moved to Live Oak in August of that year. Her mother, Monteen Lillian Beck Moore, was twenty-seven at the time of her birth.

Barbara's birth was not an easy one. Dr. J. Marvin Price, longtime Live Oak physician, was called to assist. Across the street from the Viola House, another woman was also in the process of giving birth. Dr. Price had to run between the two houses throughout the night until both children were safely delivered.

The Moores lived in Live Oak for only a brief time, as Estul was transferred to another railroad location in July 1935. In July 1937, he was briefly reassigned to Live Oak. However, in January 1938, his position in Live Oak was eliminated and he was transferred to another location on the Atlantic Coast Line.

Barbara and her family eventually moved to Albany, Georgia, in 1948, where she graduated from high school in 1952. Classmates stated that she was a beautiful young woman and very popular with the boys. After high school, she attended Albany Business College for one year. After working for the Atlantic Coast Line for twenty-eight years, Barbara's father passed away on April 20, 1953, in a Brunswick, Georgia hospital, leaving behind his wife and several children.

Monteen Moore remarried, and together mother and daughter began working at Albany's Turner Air Force Base. It was there that Barbara's mother met a young Kentucky-born air force lieutenant. She introduced him to Barbara, and the two hit it off. They were engaged for two years before being married in 1955 at the Lovejoy Memorial United Methodist Church in Newnan, Georgia; Barbara's brother Jack Moore, the minister there, performed the wedding. After a honeymoon in Miami, the two returned to Albany for a time before relocating to several bases, including ones in Athens, Greece, and Tripoli, Libya.

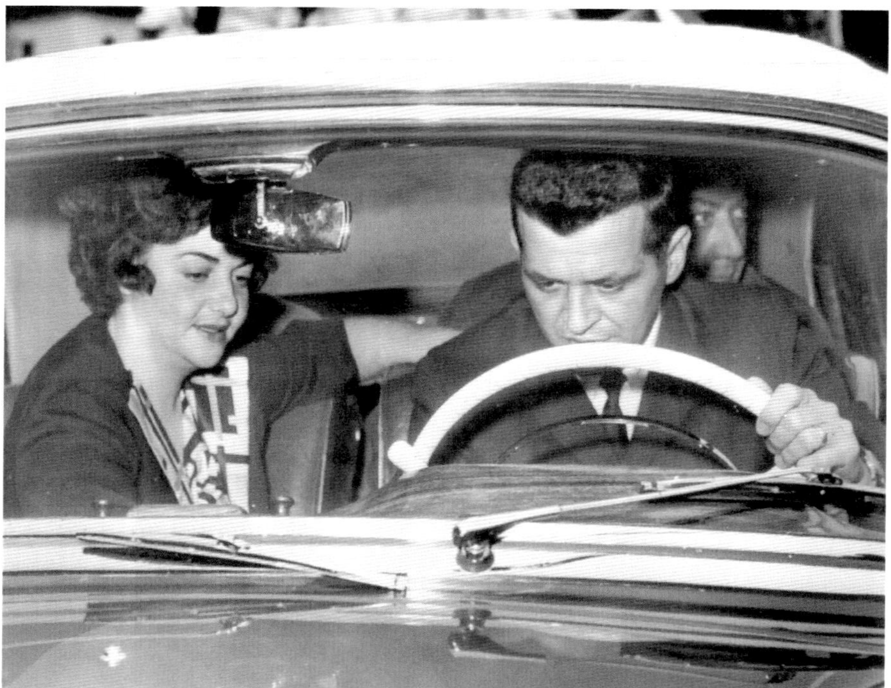

Francis Gary Powers and his wife, Barbara, after his release from Soviet captivity, 1962. *Associated Press.*

By 1960, Barbara and her husband had moved to Virginia, but her husband was often far away. Barbara herself didn't know exactly what her husband's duty was; at one point, she believed that he flew jet trainers for service and overhaul in Germany. At other times, she thought that he might be smuggling guns for revolutionaries. On May 1, 1960, Barbara's husband took off from Pakistan for one of his "routine" flights. Unbeknown to Barbara at the time, her husband was flying top-secret reconnaissance missions over the Soviet Union in a secret U-2 spy plane for the Central Intelligence Agency (with an annual income of $30,000 per year, which is nearly $250,000 in 2015 dollars). Her husband's name: Francis Gary Powers.

The USSR was aware that American aircraft were making incursions into its airspace, but until 1960 the extreme altitude at which the U-2s flew had kept them safe from harm. However, the Soviet Union had recently installed more modern missiles that could reach high altitudes, and they were ready for Powers's spy plane when it entered its airspace. Repeated attempts by fighter jets and missiles finally shot down Powers's plane (as well as one of the pursing Soviet fighters). Powers was able to bail out over Soviet territory, where he was quickly captured.

American forces quickly realized that Powers's plane had been shot down. However, as it was a top-secret mission and there was to be an international peace summit within days, a cover story was created. The official story was that the aircraft was a weather research plane whose pilot had experienced oxygen difficulties and ejected while over friendly Turkey; the aircraft had continued on autopilot until it crashed deep inside the Soviet Union.

Unfortunately for the United States, the Soviet Union had a partially intact aircraft and a living pilot in its custody. The USSR embarrassed the United States through the international media. The peace summit made no progress; the arms race accelerated and lasted until the breakup of the Soviet Union thirty years later.

Francis "Frank" Gary Powers was tried by the Soviet Union for espionage in August 1960. Live Oak–born Barbara, as well as Powers's parents, were present during the trial. Barbara appeared devoted to Francis during the long ordeal, vowing to stay in Moscow until "I've done everything possible" to have her husband released, hiring her own attorney separate from her in-laws' lawyer. Powers was found guilty and sentenced to three years in prison and seven years of hard labor. Before Barbara returned to the United States, Soviet authorities allowed her one hour with her husband behind closed doors.

Two years later, in February 1962, Powers was released from Soviet captivity in exchange for a captured Soviet spy. Powers would later state, "I was a pilot flying an airplane and it just so happened that, where I was flying, made what I was doing spying." Powers appeared before the Senate Armed Services Committee to answer questions about the ordeal; oddly enough, Barbara was not present with him, nor for the Virginia homecoming that followed. She stated that she had personal affairs to settle at her mother's home in Georgia. Barbara's mother would later declare, "Barbara hasn't been herself since Gary was shot down."

In August 1962, only six months after Powers's release from a Soviet prison and return to America, he filed for divorce from Barbara on the grounds of cruelty and intoxication. He charged her with "habitual intoxication" and claimed that she cursed and abused him without cause. Powers further added that he and Barbara had been separated since May 27 of that year and that, in April, she had overdosed on sleeping pills and been admitted to a hospital for three days. It did not help Barbara's cause that she was nicknamed "Gay Barbie" because of her alcoholic behavior at the officers' club over the years. Powers himself later wrote that he had suffered more from Barbara's torture than he had from Soviet interrogations and prison!

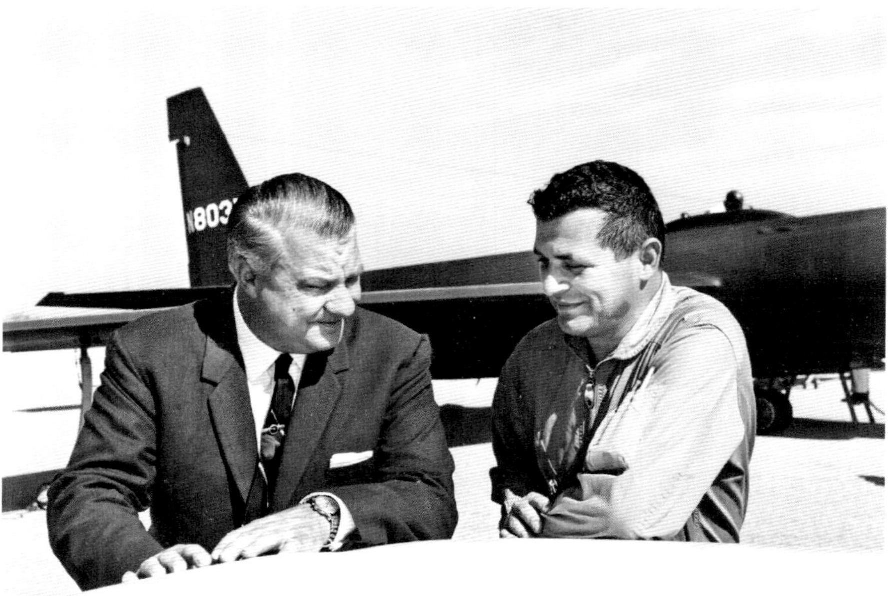

Francis Gary Powers talking with U-2 designer Kelly Johnson in 1966. *United States Air Force.*

The divorce was finalized, and Powers moved on with his life, marrying again in 1963 to a CIA psychologist named Claudia Sue Edwards Downey. She debriefed pilots upon their return from foreign missions. The couple would have one son, Francis Gary Powers Jr., and a daughter, Dee. Powers himself would die in a civilian helicopter crash in 1977.

As for Barbara, she returned to Albany, Georgia, and worked at a marine corps logistics base, which she later sued for unfair labor practices. It was determined by a judge that the base had violated Barbara's right to have a union representative present at an interview likely to result in disciplinary action against her.

Barbara eventually retired from the marine corps logistics base in Albany as an inventory management specialist. She died at her home on April 7, 2014, at the age of seventy-nine, leaving behind husband Charles F. Steward, a daughter, several grandchildren and one great-grandchild.

Barbara Moore was in the international spotlight for a brief time during an important period of American history, when the world could have seen a nuclear holocaust. Her Live Oak roots have been all but forgotten, yet the information quietly resides in the records of the Suwannee County Clerk's Office today.

PART II

# FADED MEMORIES

# 7

# "EDUCATION IS THE KEY TO UNLOCK THE GOLDEN DOOR OF FREEDOM"

## *African American Schools of Higher Learning*

*Education is the key to unlock the golden door of freedom.*
*—George Washington Carver*

Suwannee County has been the home of thousands of hardworking Americans over the years. Many times, these individuals help make their communities and the surrounding area better places in which to live. Sometimes, however, they are able to reach far beyond the local community and enter the state and national stage. Such were those leaders who established schools of higher learning in Suwannee County.

African American education expanded soon after the end of the Civil War. Suwannee County's original Douglass School, named for famed African American abolitionist Frederick Douglass, was established in 1868 or 1869 (depending on the source). The school was first located on Houston Street and was open from June through September. In 1927, a newer structure was built nearby on the same street, partially funded by Julius Rosenwald, the American businessman and philanthropist who established a fund in his name to support African American education in the rural South.

In 1950, construction began on the first phase of the school campus that eventually became the "new" Douglass School on Ontario Avenue. The campus was substantially completed by 1956, with a gymnasium added in 1965. There was even some discussion of the campus housing an African American junior college for the region; instead, the college was built in neighboring Madison as the Suwannee River Junior College (it merged with

North Florida Junior College in 1966; the college is now known as North Florida Community College). The Douglass School was used as such until 1969, when desegregation occurred. The school then became the Suwannee Middle School until the present Suwannee Middle School was completed in 1990 on South Walker Street. The former African American school was renamed the Douglass Center and has been used as an alternative school, a Boys' and Girls' Club and other related institutions since that time.

The Douglass School saw several notable graduates in its history, including some with a connection to American civil rights history. For instance, Arnold Waters and Juanita Howard, both 1968 graduates of Douglas High School, married and had a daughter named Andrea. In 2006, Andrea married Martin Luther King III, son of prominent civil rights leader Dr. Martin Luther King Jr. and a national community activist in his own right.

## THE FLORIDA INSTITUTE

However, Douglass High School was not the only African American institute of learning established in Suwannee County during Reconstruction. In 1873, the Florida Bethlehem Baptist Theological Institute, a group of African American leaders who wished to create a school of learning for other African Americans, purchased the Live Oak White Male and Female Seminary from Elijah F. Henderson. The building itself had almost served as the Suwannee County Courthouse not once, but two times, but ultimately the proposals had fallen through. The school finally opened to African American students in 1880, after the end of Reconstruction. It was usually called the Florida Baptist Institute or Florida Institute. In 1916, with the completion of a new school building for white students, the Suwannee County School Board authorized the Florida Institute to take possession of and move the original part of the 1889 wood school building that had served white students; this school had been the first public school in Live Oak. The old structure would be used as dormitories for Florida Institute students for several decades.

In 1918, the Florida Institute added a two-year college program and became Florida Memorial College. After serving as such for many years, the institute merged with the St. Augustine–based Florida Normal and Industrial Institute in 1941, becoming the Florida Normal and Industrial Memorial College. The college later became Florida Memorial College and is currently Florida Memorial University, one of the oldest African American

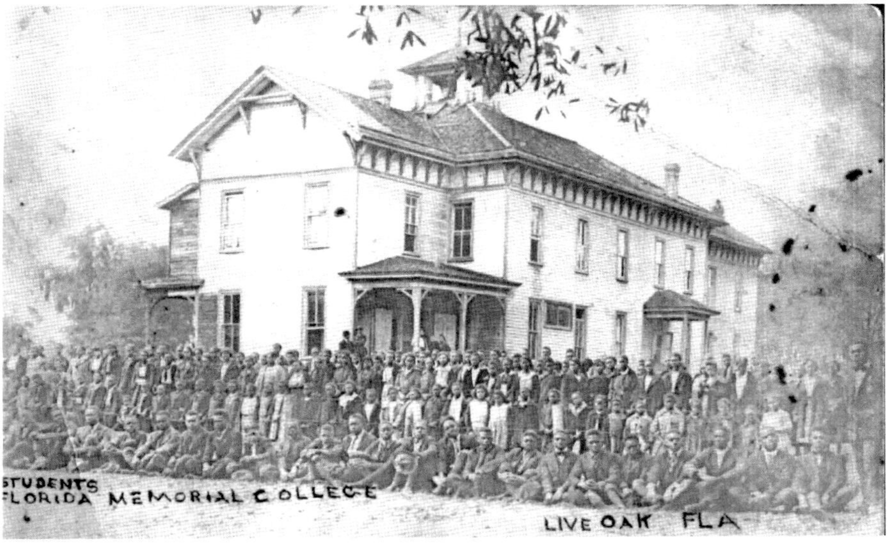


Students of Florida Memorial College in front of a building that formerly was the first white public high school in Live Oak and later obtained by the college, circa 1920. *Suwannee County Historical Museum.*

universities in the state of Florida. The old school structures left behind in Live Oak were eventually sold at public auction and torn down to make way for Suwannee County's first public hospital in 1948. That hospital was torn down in the 1990s and replaced with the Azalea Court subdivision.

## HARRY T. MOORE

One of the Florida Institute's most famous students was Suwannee County native Harry T. Moore. Harry Tyson Moore was born on November 18, 1905, in the community of Houston, one-time county seat of Suwannee County. He was the only child of Johnny and Rosa Moore, and his middle name came from his mother's maiden name. Harry's father kept the water tanks full for the railroad that ran through Houston and operated a small store in the front of the Moore home. Unfortunately, Johnny Moore's health began to decline in 1914, and he died later that year. Rosa worked in the cotton fields and ran the little store to try to make ends meet, but things were difficult. In 1915, Rosa sent Harry to live with one of her sisters in Daytona

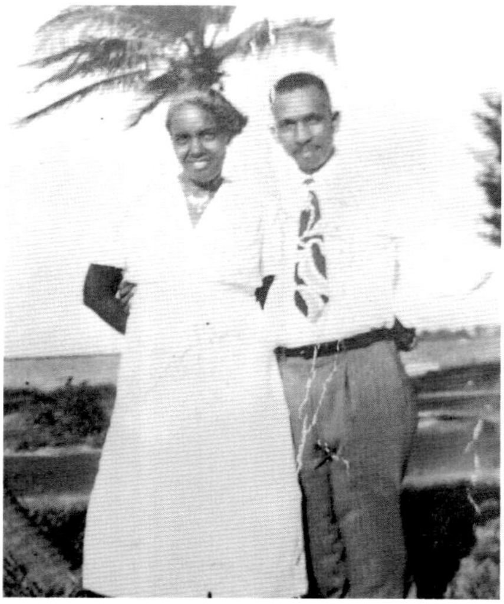

Harry T. and Harriette Moore, circa 1950. *State Archives of Florida.*

Beach. In 1916, Harry moved to Jacksonville and until 1919 lived with three of his aunts.

Despite being away from his mother, Harry's life in Jacksonville had its advantages. The city was one of the largest in the state, and there was a large and active community of African Americans. Harry's three aunts were all educated women (two were teachers and the third a nurse), allowing him to have a more varied experience than he would have received had he remained in Houston. This exposure would stimulate Harry's love of learning and education that would last the rest of his life.

In 1919, Harry T. Moore returned home to Suwannee County and entered Florida Memorial College in Live Oak. Harry did well in school, earning straight As (except for one B+). His peers nicknamed him "Doc" because of his studious behavior. On graduating in May 1925 with a "normal" degree (a degree program to train teachers), he began teaching in the town of Cocoa at the only African American elementary school there.

Harry met Harriette Simms while in Cocoa, and within a year, they were married; two daughters would be born to them by 1930. Harry and Harriette moved to Mims, a small town outside of Titusville where Harriette's parents lived. Harry was soon promoted to principal of the Titusville Colored School.

In 1934, Harry T. Moore entered the spotlight when he founded the Brevard County chapter of the National Association for the Advancement of Colored People (NAACP). This was the first of more than fifty NAACP branches that Moore would eventually establish in Florida. Three years after founding the Brevard chapter, Moore filed the first lawsuit in the Deep South to equalize white and African American teacher salaries. Although he lost the case, it spurred other federal lawsuits in Florida that would eventually lead to equal salaries.

By 1941, Moore was totally focused on his NAACP work. That year, he organized the Florida State Conference of the NAACP and served as its executive secretary. Although he began his quest for equality with a focus on unequal salaries, segregated schools and the lack of African American voters, by 1943, Moore was focusing on lynchings and law enforcement brutality. He threw himself into the work with gusto, obtaining sworn affidavits from victims' families and making his own investigations. From that point until his death, Moore investigated every single lynching in Florida.

In 1944, Moore organized the Progressive Voters' League to assist with registering Florida African Americans to vote. Within six years, he had helped to register over 116,000 African Americans; this represented more than 31 percent of all eligible African American voters and was a much higher percentage than any other state in the South. However, Moore suffered from his activism, and in 1946, both he and his wife were let go from their teaching jobs. Moore became a full-time, paid organizer of the Florida NAACP.

In July 1949, four young African American men were accused and found guilty of raping a white woman in the community of Groveland in Lake County. Moore investigated the charges and found evidence that the defendants had been beaten severely; Moore blamed Sheriff Willis McCall. The evidence against the four men was sketchy, inducing the U.S. Supreme Court to overturn the convictions and order a new trial. On November 6, 1951, Sheriff McCall was driving two of the men back to Lake County for a pretrial hearing when he shot them, killing one and severely wounding the other. McCall claimed that the two handcuffed prisoners had attacked him while trying to escape. The survivor countered that the sheriff had shot them in cold blood. A national scandal ensued, and Harry T. Moore called for Sheriff McCall's suspension and indictment for murder.

Six weeks later, on December 25, 1951, Harry T. Moore and his wife celebrated Christmas and their twenty-fifth wedding anniversary before going to bed. A few hours later, a massive explosion rocked their Mims home; a bomb had been planted directly beneath their bedroom. The force of the explosion pushed the Moores' heavy bed through the ceiling rafters. Harry Moore died on the way to the hospital; Harriette died nine days later of massive internal injuries. Harry T. Moore was the first prominent civil rights leader to be assassinated, and he is considered the first martyr of the civil rights movement.

Today, many decades after the murders, the case remains officially unsolved. After several FBI investigations and a 2005–06 inquest by the State of Florida, the most reasonable explanation was that at least four violent members of the Central Florida Ku Klux Klan were involved.

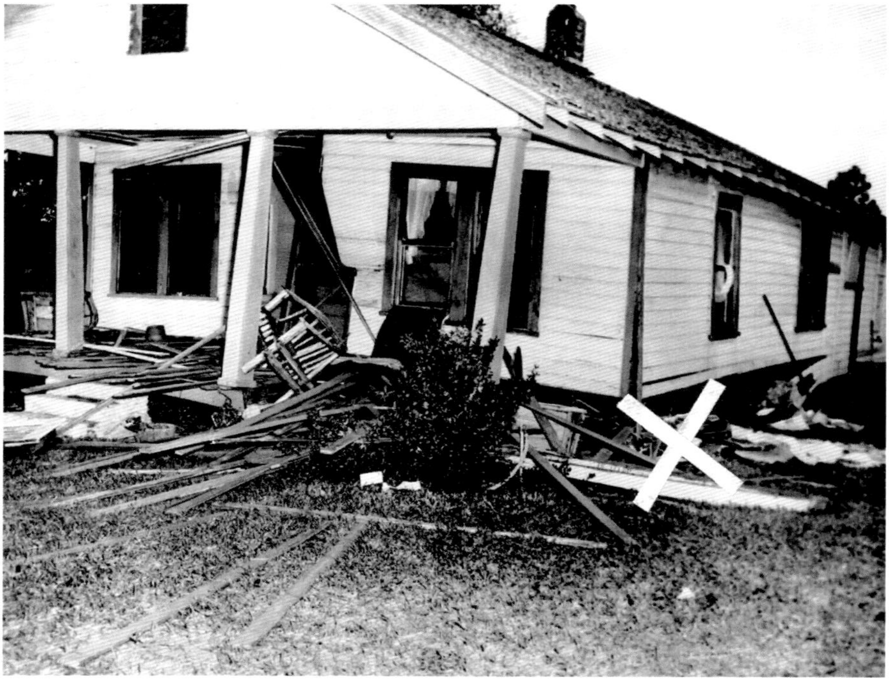

The home of Harry and Harriette Moore after the bombing, December 1951. *State Archives of Florida.*

These men were investigated in the years following the bombing. Two of the men died within a year of the bombing of natural causes, and a third committed suicide in 1952 after being grilled by the FBI about the case. The last probable bomber died of cancer in 1978.

Unfortunately, Harry T. Moore would not be the last martyr of the civil rights movement. Along with Moore, people such as Medgar Evers, Martin Luther King Jr. and dozens of others would pay the ultimate price for their quest for equality.

## BROWN'S THEOLOGICAL SEMINARY

The Florida Institute was not the only school for higher learning located in Suwannee County. In 1870, the African Methodist Episcopal Church Conference held a meeting in Quincy to determine a suitable site for an

African American college. Live Oak was chosen as the best location due to its junction of east–west and north–south railroads, but little was done for the next two years. However, the realization that a Baptist institution (the Florida Institute) was being erected spurred additional activity. A ten-acre tract was purchased on March 5, 1872, from Nancy Parshley near the current John Hale Park for the construction of what came to be called the Brown Theological Seminary, or Brown's Theological and Classical Institute. On July 4 of that year, construction of the institute began with great fanfare when a crowd of one thousand people attended the laying of the cornerstone.

In 1873, the school was renamed Brown's University of the State of Florida, but the main building was still incomplete. A series of scandals, fires, financial panics, embezzlement and, finally, a hurricane all but destroyed the will to continue the almost-completed school building. Ultimately, the carpenters sued the trustees for past wages and won the lawsuit, ending construction of Brown's University in Live Oak for good. The nearly complete building was sold to the highest bidder and dismantled. In 1883, the school reopened in Jacksonville and was soon renamed Edward Waters College, continuing today as the oldest private college in the state of Florida.

For more than sixty years, through the efforts of forward-thinking whites and African Americans, Suwannee County, and Live Oak in particular, was a center of learning for the oft-neglected African American community. Although Suwannee County no longer contains dedicated African American schools of higher learning within its boundaries, the county continues to benefit from its educational history.

# 8

# "WHAT'S IN A NAME?"

## *Suwannee County Streets*

As one travels through local communities and passes by the various streets and roads, he or she may ask, "Where did that street's name originate?" Fortunately for Suwannee County, there are many streets (some of which no longer exist) that have rich and varied histories. Learning about the origins of these street names will also help one to learn a little bit more about the people and events that have shaped Suwannee County's history.

### Conner Street

One of the first streets in Live Oak, Conner Street is named after the Conner family. The probable namesake is Nelson Conner, who moved to the vicinity around the time of the Civil War. Nelson Conner was a preacher, businessman and Suwannee County's second clerk of the court. His Conner Hotel on East Conner Street fronted the railroad, providing weary travelers a convenient place to rest. Conner was partially responsible for the transfer of the county seat from Houston to Live Oak but probably used underhanded methods in his quest after a gentlemen's agreement with John Parshley. Parshley agreed to give Conner the deeds to certain property on Howard and Church Streets if Conner would campaign to have the county seat moved from Houston to Live Oak and construct a courthouse on land donated by the Parshleys across the street from his house on Ohio Avenue.

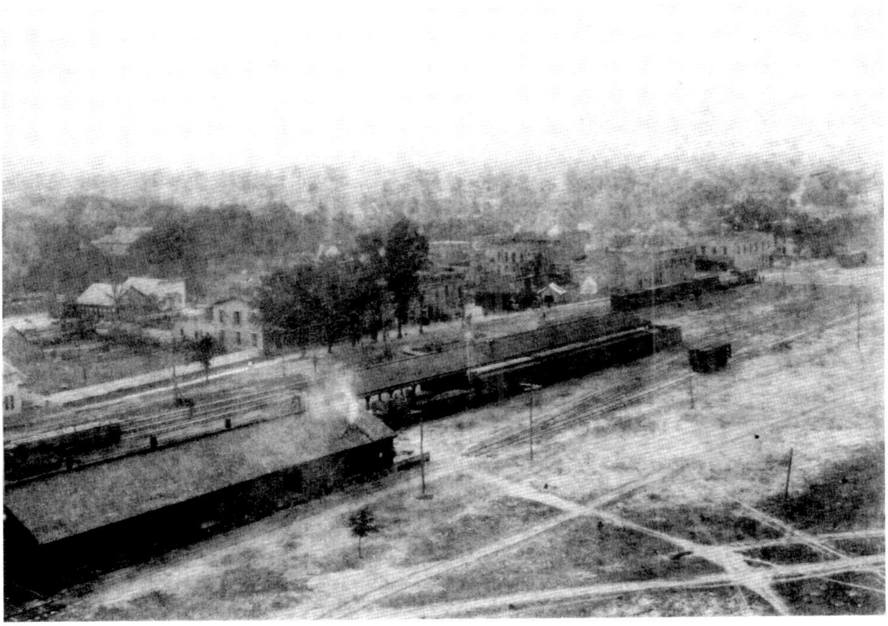

A view of Conner Street from the Live Oak water tower, looking roughly west. The Ethel House is situated behind the row of trees near the picture's center, and the Live Oak House is barely visible in the top right. The photograph was taken between 1897 and 1903. *Suwannee County Historical Museum.*

Conner was also the man responsible for physically moving the Baptist church to the Parshley site (present-day location of the courthouse) when the county purchased the building in 1869 for use as a courthouse. Conner did not properly secure the building, and it blew down in a storm just before the Suwannee County commissioners' meeting on May 13, 1870. Needing money, Nelson Conner blackmailed Nancy Parshley for the deeds to the Howard and Church Street properties based on a gentleman's agreement with Parshley. Nancy Parshley tearfully handed over the deeds and then promptly sued for blackmail. Conner died in February 1871; it is possible that the stress of the lawsuit and resulting public scandal had something to do with it. Nancy Parshley ended up with much of Conner's estate due to the financial trouble in which Conner's family then found themselves.

Nelson Conner's son J.N. (Jesse Nelson) would redeem the family's name, becoming a county judge for Suwannee County in 1893 and serving until 1919. Various other family members would make a positive mark on the county's history, as well.

Portions of Conner Street were at different times in Live Oak's history called Railroad Street and Fourth Street. Its row of boardinghouses and hotels, such as the Ethel Hotel and Live Oak House, were well known to railroad travelers in the late 1800s.

## DOWLING STREET

Dowling Street in Live Oak is named for Thomas Dowling, prominent Live Oak and Suwannee County citizen in the late 1800s and early 1900s. Born in Hamilton County in 1851, he operated a lumber mill in Lake City before moving his operations to Suwannee County around 1888. There, he constructed a large lumber mill and planing mill on the east side of Live Oak. In an attempt to increase his fortune during the heyday of railroads in the area, he helped form the Live Oak, Luraville & Deadman's Bay Railroad Company. In the 1890s, Dowling and his family constructed the R.L. Dowling Short Line Railroad for their Live Oak sawmills, which gradually expanded to reach the community of Hudson. Hudson was soon renamed Dowling Park after the influential family. In 1906, Dowling Short Line was incorporated as the Live Oak, Perry & Gulf Railroad (popularly known as the "Loping Gopher") to serve the Dowling family's sawmill and

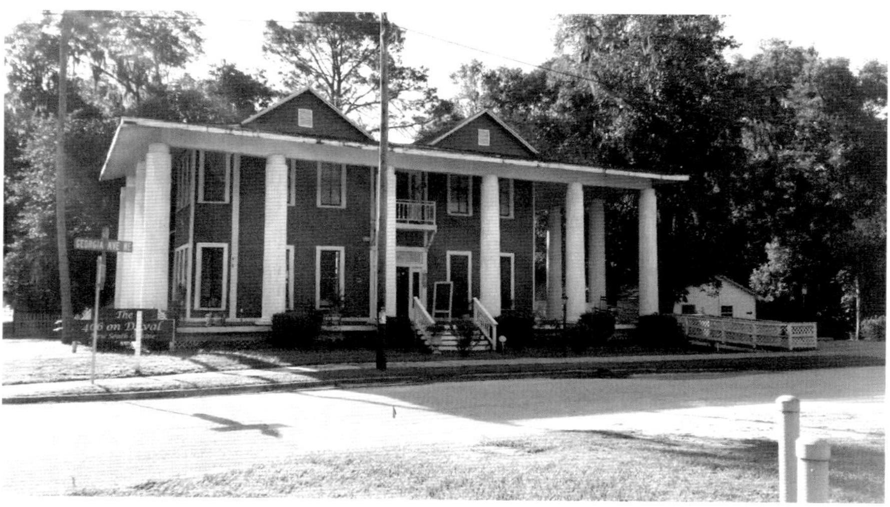

Home of Thomas Dowling in Live Oak, 2016. *Author's collection.*

later freight and passenger traffic. Thomas Dowling's sawmill was one of the two largest in Florida at the time (the other was also located within Suwannee County).

Thomas Dowling also began Live Oak's first waterworks in 1897, paid for from his own resources (and coincidentally built across the street from his mansion on Duval Street). He was instrumental in selling property that would become the Advent Christian Village before his death in 1911.

## DUVAL STREET

Although we cannot determine with 100 percent certainty the origin of the name "Duval Street" in Live Oak, it must be assumed that it is named after Duval County, which in turn was named after William Pope Duval (also spelled "DuVal"), early governor of Florida. The street's name hearkens back to the years of American occupation of Florida nearly two hundred years ago, when men and women carved Suwannee County and its first communities from the native pine and live oak forests, fighting diseases and Native Americans who still roamed the countryside.

William Pope Duval was born in Virginia in 1784, the son of a Revolutionary War officer. His grandfather had been in the Virginia House of Burgesses and was present when Patrick Henry gave his famous "Give me liberty or give me death!" speech. The youngest child, Duval left home at fourteen to become a hunter in Kentucky but soon began to study law. During an outbreak of hostilities with Indians in 1812, Duval was given command of mounted volunteer troops. Shortly thereafter, he was elected to the U.S. Congress, where he served until 1815. Choosing not to seek reelection, he returned to Kentucky and continued to practice law.

In 1821, East and West Florida became territories of the United States, and Duval was named the first U.S. judge for the East Florida district of the superior court on May 18. The Suwannee River was the dividing line between East and West Florida. Shortly thereafter, East and West Florida were consolidated into the single territory of Florida, and the former territories of East and West Florida became known as St. Johns and Escambia Counties. On April 17, 1822, President James Monroe appointed Duval as the first nonmilitary governor of Florida, succeeding General Andrew Jackson. He served for twelve years as the territorial governor, being reappointed by Presidents John Quincy Adams and Andrew Jackson. Among his accomplishments was the relocation of the capital to Tallahassee, dealing peacefully with the Native Americans through actions such as the Treaty at Moultrie Creek and establishing the local court system and the clerk of the circuit court, as well as many of the other basic services that continue to be provided to Floridians. He was noted for his wit and humorous stories, could write in both French and Spanish and was a great speaker.

William Duval continued to live in Florida for a number of years, continuing his practice of law. In 1838, he was a member of the constitutional convention that met in St. Joseph, where Suwannee County (at the time part of Columbia County) native George McClellan was one of the delegates. Duval was also a member of the territorial senate from 1839 to 1842. In 1845, he served as a commissioner to help settle the disputed northern boundary of Florida, which was the same year that he became the first grand master of the Masonic Grand Lodge of Florida. He moved to Texas in 1848 with his wife and eight children to continue practicing law; Sam Houston was among his clients. Duval's 375-acre plantation in Tallahassee later became the site of Florida A&M University. He died in 1854 in Washington, D.C., and was buried at the Congressional Cemetery there. He has been celebrated in fiction by James K. Paulding, who portrayed him as "Nimrod Wildfire" in his play *The Lion of the West*, and by Washington Irving, who based his character Ralph Ringwood on Duval after traveling with him by stagecoach. Even Ralph Waldo Emerson wrote of the governor, saying that he was "the button on which all things are hung." It has been said that Duval would have been very wealthy if he had not given away the majority of his fortune to charity.

Duval County was created in 1822 out of a portion of St. Johns County, one of the two original counties. It stretched from the Suwannee River to the Atlantic Ocean and from the mouth of the Suwannee River north to the Florida-Georgia line, encompassing present-day Suwannee County, as well as several other modern-day counties.

Duval Street in Live Oak has existed since before 1885, when it appeared on the first known insurance map of the community. At that date, there were already a variety of stores and homes along both sides of the street, indicating a much earlier establishment. A detailed search of the records of the city and county would doubtless find earlier references to the street. For many years, Duval Street was a main thoroughfare into Live Oak, reaching to White Springs via what was called the White Springs Road outside of the city limits (now County Road 136). In some maps of Live Oak west of Ohio Avenue, portions of Duval Street are also called Third Street.

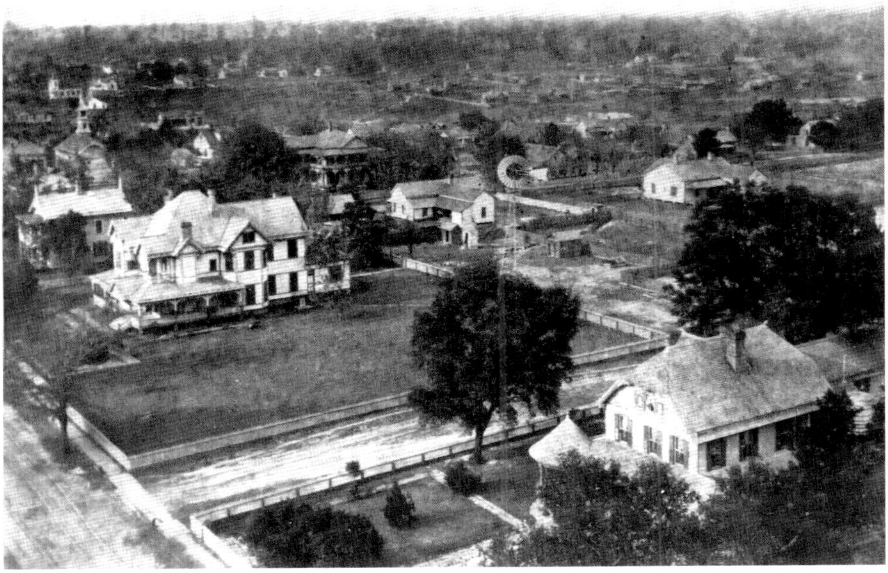

Photograph of Duval Street around 1900. The homes of several prominent citizens line Duval Street, and other stately homes are visible in the background. *Suwannee County Historical Museum.*

In the first years of the twentieth century, when Live Oak was one of the largest cities in the state, Duval Street was lined with dozens of two- and three-story homes of the wealthiest families in Suwannee County. Although many of these stately homes and their families are now gone, several still remain. Duval Street has a rich legacy that is equaled by few streets within Suwannee County.

## HAINES STREET

Henry Stevens Haines was born in Nantucket, Massachusetts, on November 21, 1836. However, his parents were from the South and he lived much of his early life in Savannah, Georgia. He married Elizabeth J. Owens of Charleston, South Carolina, when he was twenty-one. Owens was the sister of C.D. Owens, a railroad official who had a Suwannee River steamboat named for him. When Elizabeth died of illness, Haines married Anna H. Davies, the daughter of the Protestant Episcopal bishop of Michigan, in the late 1890s. Both marriages produced children.

Henry Haines entered the railroad business at an early age and quickly excelled. According to one biographer, within a few short years, Haines could lay track, run an engine, repair a boiler, issue payroll and balance books, all in the same morning. It was not long before he became superintendent of the Charleston & Savannah Railroad. Because of his experience, the Confederate army commissioned him as a colonel during the Civil War, placing him in charge of maintaining military transportation service in North and South Carolina.

After the Civil War, Haines took a position as general superintendent of the failing Atlantic & Gulf Railroad, which had a connector line running between Live Oak and Lawton, Georgia. This railroad, in conjunction with the Pensacola & Georgia Railroad, accessed Jacksonville to Tallahassee and beyond. The junction through Live Oak linked Florida to the rest of the country. Within six years, he had turned the company around, but a failed cotton crop nearly bankrupted the company. Still hanging on, Haines continued for another six years until the Atlantic & Gulf Railroad finally went into receivership in 1878 due to unpaid loans. Henry Plant, owner of the Southern Express Company and soon to be a famous Florida entrepreneur, purchased the railroad in an 1879 auction for $300,000. The purchase of this railroad was the first of many for Plant, and he named Henry Haines general superintendent of the new line. The railroad was renamed the Savannah, Florida & Western Railway, but it was popularly dubbed the "Plant System" after its owner. Among the railroad's depot stops was the town of Live Oak.

Colonel Henry Haines quickly became Plant's go-to man, heading up railroad work throughout the Southeast. For the time, Haines continued with his office in Savannah, developing various industrial and business methods used for many decades. In his obituary, he was credited, among other things, with introducing the naval stores industry to Savannah. Eventually, Haines's natural leadership abilities led him to be promoted to vice president of the Plant System with his office in New York. He continued to show an active interest in the welfare of Savannah, however, and always called the city his home.

One of Colonel Haines's greatest achievements was to establish the Plant System's Tampa-Havana Steamship Line in 1883–84. Haines, with limited time and working in the rainiest part of the season in a region dense with wetlands, swamps and forests, was able to lay seventy miles of track to extend Plant's railroad from Tampa to Sanford. This connection made it possible for Plant's steamship line to connect with the rest of his railroad holdings all the way up the East Coast of the United States and confirmed Plant's dominance in the railroad industry. It also spurred growth in places like Orlando, Tampa and Lakeland. Today's Interstate 4 generally follows the original route taken by the Sanford-Tampa Line. One of the locations affected by Haines's work was the village of Clay Cut, which in his honor was renamed Haines City.

After also serving as general manager of the Plant System's line of steamships on the St. Johns River, Colonel Haines finally retired from the railroad business in 1894 in order to travel throughout Europe. During his retirement, he wrote several books concerning railroads and was considered one of the world's leading experts in the field until his death. Two of his most popular works were *American Railway Management*, published in 1897, and *Problems in Railroad Regulation*, published in 1911. Colonel Haines served as president of the American Society of Civil Engineers and the American Society of Mechanical Engineers and was a member of the Railway Guild.

After a long life (especially in light of his strenuous work schedule), Colonel Henry Stevens Haines passed away on November 3, 1923, in Lenox, Massachusetts; he was almost eighty-seven years old. Haines was buried in Savannah.

Close to the railroad near the center of Live Oak, its citizens paid tribute to Colonel Henry Haines by naming the first street north of the railroad after him; it shows up on maps before 1885 and is aptly adjacent to the passenger and freight depots. It was a fitting honor for a man indirectly responsible for Live Oak's growth as a railroad hub of north Florida in the mid- to late 1800s.

The Town of Branford also named one of its major streets after Colonel Haines.

## HOUSTON STREET

Houston Street was one of Live Oak's first streets, and those who first settled in Live Oak did so where Houston Street intersects with the east–west railroad (originally the Pensacola & Georgia Railroad and now CSX

Transportation). In other words, it was the first "downtown" Live Oak. Houston Street is most likely named for Edward Houston (also spelled Houstoun), president of the Pensacola & Georgia Railroad when Live Oak was established in 1859 (or shortly thereafter). He is also the probable namesake for the community of Houston, which was Suwannee County's first permanent county seat (after the original temporary seat of "the house of William Hines") from 1859 to 1868.

## HOWARD STREET

Howard Street in Live Oak is named for John Howard Parshley, one of the sons of John and Nancy Parshley. John Parshley, originally from New York but later from Massachusetts and Ohio, moved to Live Oak in 1866 to rebuild his fortune. Noticing the stands of immense virgin timber, he purchased property in Live Oak and established a planing mill and sawmill in conjunction with Nathan Walker. Parshley's family, including their son John Howard (who went by "Howard"), moved in 1867 to Live Oak, where

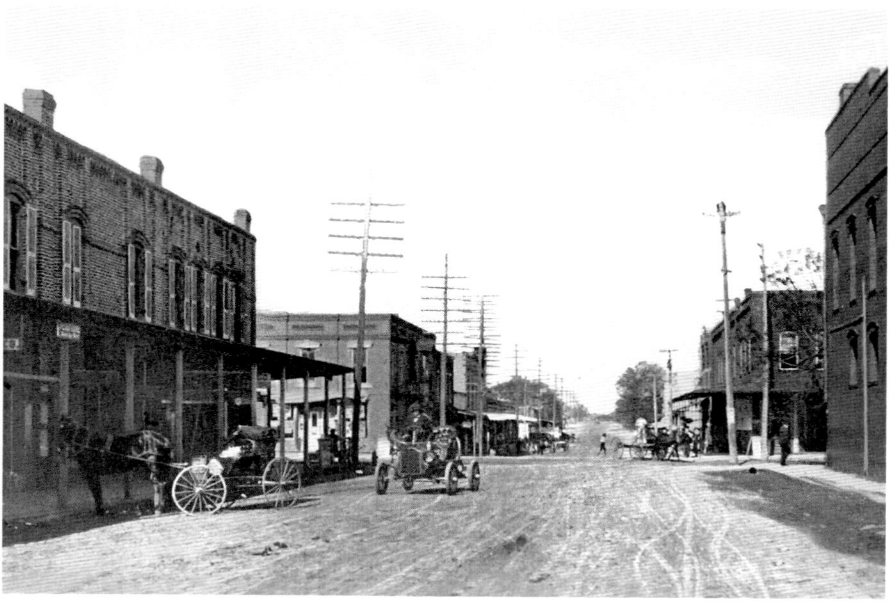

Howard Street looking west at intersection with Ohio Avenue, circa 1910. *Suwannee County Clerk of Court.*

they resided for many years. Howard Parshley later moved away from Suwannee County to pursue the ministry and died on September 4, 1907, in Bridgewater, Massachusetts. His brother Wilbur also became a minister.

## IRWIN (IRVIN) STREET

Irvin Street (also called Irwin Street) is another of Live Oak's oldest thoroughfares. The street is undoubtedly named after the Irvine family of settlers. One candidate is Colonel Washington Lafayette Irvine, who owned property in and around Live Oak and is known for having established a ferry (Irvine's Ferry) just downriver from present-day Luraville around 1870. It appears that Irvin Street originally led to Irvine's Ferry, hence a possibility for the name.

Another equally plausible source for Irvin Street's name is John A. Irvine. John and his wife, Roxanne, owned the 640 acres on which the town of Live Oak was originally chartered, before selling it to John and Nancy Parshley after the Civil War.

## OHIO AVENUE

Ohio Avenue, one of Live Oak's oldest streets, is named for the state of Ohio, from which early settler John Parshley moved in 1866. Parshley would soon lay out the streets of downtown Live Oak as we know it, with Ohio Avenue being one of the first. From that time onward, Ohio Avenue has been a

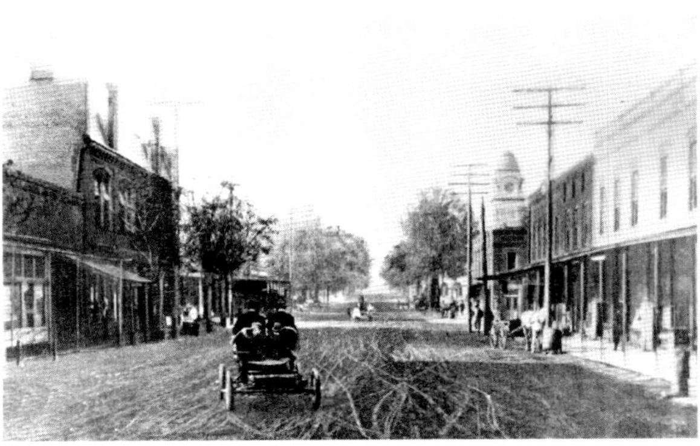

Ohio Avenue looking south toward the main intersection with Howard Street, 1906 or 1907. *Suwannee County Historical Museum.*

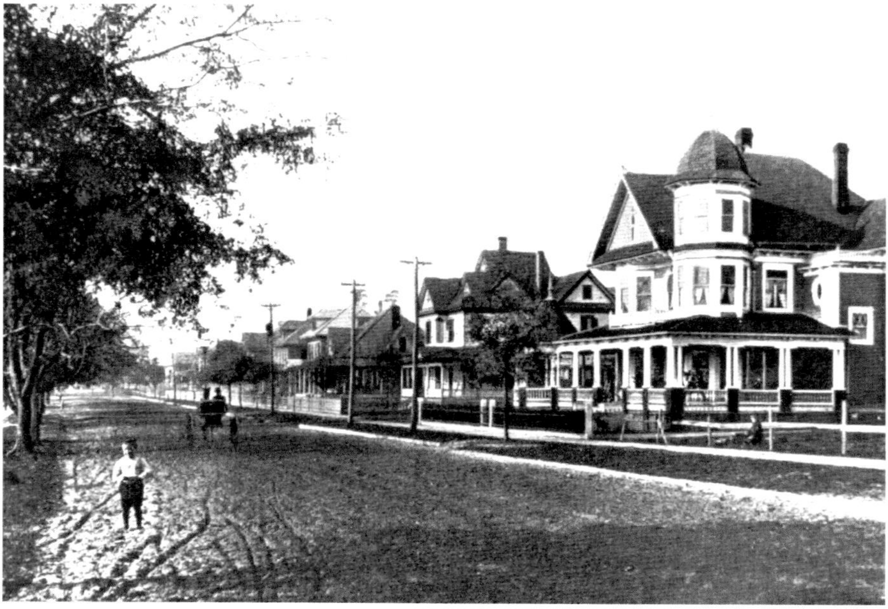

A line of majestic homes on Ohio Avenue south of the downtown area, 1906. *Suwannee County Historical Museum.*

fixture in Live Oak. It remains the primary north–south thoroughfare into and through the city of Live Oak.

In the first years of the twentieth century, Ohio Avenue was lined with dozens of magnificent live oak trees and magnificent homes of the wealthiest residents in the community. Over time, many of the houses fell into disrepair and were torn down and replaced with businesses. The live oak trees were cut down when the street was widened in the middle of the twentieth century.

## Plant Avenue

Plant Avenue in Branford is named for Henry Bradford Plant, railroad magnate and close friend of Branford founder Robert Ivey. Henry Plant was born in Branford, Connecticut, in 1819. His father died when he was six years old, and within a few years, Henry had a job as a steamer's cabin boy. Later, Plant would learn the package express business, and by the

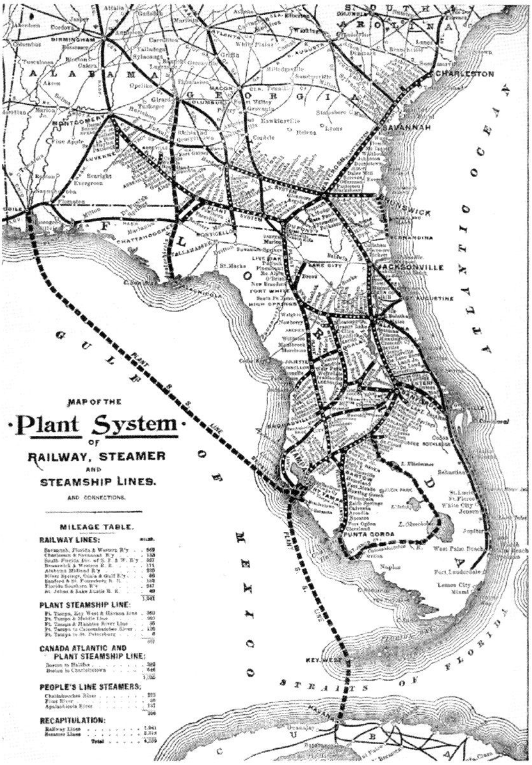


Plant System in 1895, showing railroads, steamer and steamship lines. *Georgia's Railroad History and Heritage, www.railga.com.*

1850s, he was running the New York office of the Adams Express Company. His wife's ill health forced them to move to Jacksonville for the winter, leading Plant to become superintendent of the southern part of the Adams Express Company with headquarters in Augusta, Georgia. He developed transportation contacts and knowledge of railroad and steamboat services that would serve him well the rest of his life.

When the Civil War broke out, the Adams Company sold its southern assets to Plant, fearing that they would be confiscated by the Confederate government. Plant organized the assets under the Southern Express Company. Despite his desire that war be avoided, he went to Jefferson Davis and proposed that his company handle the Confederacy's payrolls and currency shipments in return for freely transporting packages to Confederate soldiers. Davis liked Plant's candor and agreed to the request. Plant's business sense made him rich during the war.

At the end of the war, a widowed Plant (his wife had died in 1863) knew that the South would rebuild, and the key to it would be transportation.

He began buying up bankrupt railroad companies. The Savannah, Florida & Western Railway was the name of Henry Plant's reorganization of the bankrupt Charleston & Savannah Railroad after he purchased it in 1879. The SF&W expanded its holdings through the leasing or outright purchasing of other railroads throughout the Southeast.

The Savannah, Florida & Western Railway was part of the Plant System, the unofficial name given to the vast holdings of Henry Plant that included not just railroads but also steamboats and hotels. When Plant died in 1899 at the age of eighty, he was buried in his birthplace of Branford, Connecticut. His railroad empire was sold to the Atlantic Coast Line Railroad for $46.5 million; with over 2,200 miles of track, it was the largest railroad system in operation in the nineteenth century.

## Scriven Avenue

One of Live Oak's oldest streets, Scriven Avenue was probably named after Dr. John P. Screven (1827–1900), president of a number of railroads in south Georgia and also mayor of Savannah, Georgia. Dr. Screven was president of the railroad that constructed the Live Oak to Lawton (now DuPont) connection at the end of the Civil War, which opened Live Oak to a great influx of settlers after the war—for several years, anyone traveling into Florida via railroad had to come through Live Oak. What better way for Live Oak to remember the president of the railroad that brought in so much industry and citizenry than to name a street after him?

## Walker Street

Walker Street in Live Oak is named for Nathan H. Walker, a business associate of John Parshley who moved to Suwannee County after the Civil War (along with his wife, Nancy) and owned property along the street later named for him. Nathan Horace Walker was born in 1823 in "Dichton" (Dighton), Massachusetts. He was the son of Nathan and Sally Walker. By 1841, the family had moved to Ohio. On December 30, 1845, Nathan married Nancy S. Emerson of Stockport, Ohio, who was born in 1824. Nathan became a lumber merchant, dealing mainly in black walnut.

An 1860 census shows Nathan H. Walker living in Urbana, Ohio, with his wife, Nancy, and two children, Chesney Addison (age ten) and May (age one month and also known as Kate May); both children were born in Ohio. There was also a domestic servant named Mary "O'Donel" (from Ireland) and a carpenter's apprentice from Ohio named John Porter living in the house with the Walkers. Nathan's listed occupation was "carpenter." It is interesting to note that, like Walker, John Parshley had also lived in Massachusetts and Urbana, Ohio, before moving to Suwannee County.

John Parshley and Nathan H. Walker established a sawmill and lumberyard near the present-day First Baptist Church in Live Oak shortly after the Civil War. After John Parshley's death in 1868, his widow, Nancy, continued the operations but had a strained relationship with Nathan Walker. Walker's attempts to have the county seat moved to his property where the Azalea Park Subdivision is located (and formerly the location of the Suwannee County Hospital) were ultimately unsuccessful, although for a few months they appeared to be a reality. The building that resulted from this brief attempt of courthouse relocation eventually became a private school for white children before being sold to Elijah F. Henderson.

Nathan Walker fled "out West" to Chicago in the middle of the night of October 31/November 1, 1871, never to return to Suwannee County. Family records show that Nathan returned to Ohio, where he and his son operated a sawmill and eventually a chair factory. Nathan traveled throughout the eastern United States selling his black walnut furniture. Nathan's son Chesney married in 1872 and died in 1881, and his daughter May married George H. Palmer in 1884. Nathan Walker himself died in 1896 and was buried in Kenton, Ohio. His wife, Nancy, died on September 12, 1900, and is buried by his side.

## WILBUR STREET

Wilbur Street in Live Oak is named for Wilbur Brown Parshley, a son of John and Nancy Parshley. Wilbur Parshley received a doctorate of divinity and became a Baptist minister. He served as a missionary in Japan with his wife, Helen, for many years before returning to the United States. Dr. Parshley was the minister of the First Baptist Church of Live Oak on its

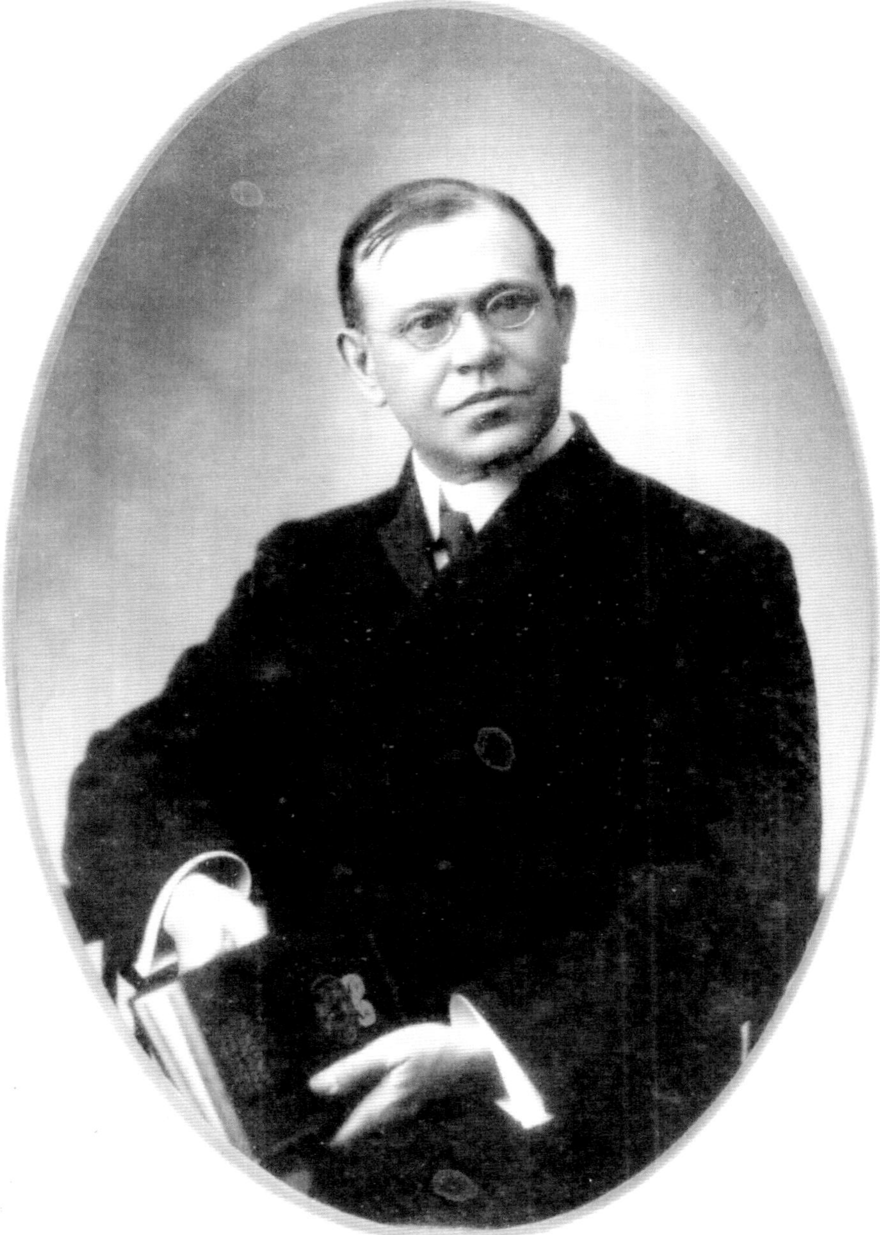

Photograph of Wilbur Parshley, circa 1900. *Thomas and Glinda Musgrove.*

fiftieth anniversary. Wilbur died on January 24, 1930, and is buried in the Live Oak Cemetery; his widow, Helen, continued to live in the Parshley Building across from the courthouse until her death in 1959. Wilbur's brother John Howard Parshley (for whom Howard Street is named) also became a minister.

## WINDERWEEDLE STREET

Winderweedle Street in Live Oak is named after B.F. (possibly Benjamin Franklin) Winderweedle (1888–1935). Winderweedle moved from Day in neighboring Lafayette County and, in 1910, began purchasing property along the current street in the Dillon and Baisden's Addition subdivisions, near the Live Oak Cemetery. Winderweedle served on the Live Oak City Council, where he was council president for part of his term. He was also an active Methodist and Mason. He was prominent in both civic and business affairs. Winderweedle passed away on June 17, 1935, at his brother's home in Tampa after having been in failing health for three years. He is buried in the Live Oak Cemetery.

9

# A MILLIONAIRE'S DREAM

## *The Hillman Bridge*

There lies an old and dilapidated bridge in the northwest corner of Suwannee County near where the current U.S. Highway 90 crosses the Suwannee River. The bridge's rusted metal trusses hearken back to one of the golden eras in Florida's history, when tourists enjoyed the newfound freedom of automobile travel to visit the Sunshine State in droves. One of the men behind the ability of automobiles to travel through Florida was W.J. Hillman, a longtime advocate for better roads. In his honor, a bridge over the Suwannee River was named the Hillman Bridge.

### W.J. Hillman

Winder Josephus Hillman was born in Warren County, Georgia, on June 19, 1857. When Hillman was still a teenager, his father died and his older brother then left for Texas to seek his fortune. Young W.J. Hillman, seeking real adventure himself, began to follow his older brother and made it to the Gulf Coast before running out of money. Speaking to a train crew, W.J. agreed to work his way west to Texas. However, when the train pulled out, it was heading east instead of west.

Hillman jumped off at the next stop, Live Oak, for a bite to eat. The train went on without him, and he had no ride. Hillman decided to settle in Live Oak and made ends meet carrying luggage from a local hotel to the train station. He then worked for the *Banner of Liberty*, one of the precursors to the current *Suwannee Democrat*. However, his printing job ended after he butchered a difficult railroad schedule.

Deciding that printing work did not suit him, Hillman began working under Major Henry Wyse and later Major Charles K. Dutton in the naval stores business. At the time (the 1870s), Suwannee County's naval stores business was one of its largest industries, and Wyse and Dutton were the two largest stakeholders in the county. The trade was so great that the State of Florida leased half of its convicts to companies in Suwannee County to work in these camps, and Hillman became a guard at one of them.

Despite some setbacks, Hillman eventually proved to be a natural leader and within eight years was in charge of over 460 convict laborers; it is during this time that he acquired his lifelong nickname of "Captain." Eventually earning enough money to open his own convict camp at High Springs, Hillman prospered until a powerful storm practically wiped out his fortunes. Hillman went to Inverness with his existing convicts and was again successful. He expanded his naval stores operations into Floral City and other locations in central and south Florida before becoming a director of the Consolidated Naval Stores Company of Jacksonville, the largest naval stores trader in the United States. Hillman remained one of the largest manufacturers of naval stores in Florida for many years and owned or operated several leading businesses in Jacksonville, where he lived for a time.

Hillman retired from the naval stores business in 1902 in his mid-forties and sold the majority of his land and interests; he did, however, keep some thirty thousand or forty thousand acres of pinelands and farms. He and his wife, Lela (they had been married on March 3, 1885), returned to Live Oak to settle down. Hillman had a large home built for him on South Ohio Avenue. His home became a showplace and exemplified the wealth found in Live Oak at a time when it was the fifth-largest city in Florida. Captain Hillman did not stay idle, however. He invested money and time in several farms within Suwannee County. Hillman was responsible for building a road to his large farm some thirteen miles south of Live Oak (he called the farm "Hillmonia"), where he conducted agricultural experiments. The road that he built was later called the Hillman Highway and is now U.S. 129, one of the major thoroughfares in Suwannee County.

According to his close friend C.N. Hildreth (a prominent resident of Live Oak), Captain Hillman was the first man in Florida to own a car. Other sources credit Thomas Dowling (of Live Oak) with this distinction. Either way, Hillman invested heavily in better roads for not only Suwannee County but also the entire state. He was one of the first stockholders of the First National Bank of Live Oak (established in 1901). When Hillman realized that Live Oak needed a modern hotel, he was one of the men who organized a company to build the Suwannee Hotel across from the Suwannee County Courthouse. The Suwannee Hotel was for many years a favorite stop for travelers before it was demolished in the mid-1970s to make way for a bank. Hillman was also vice president of the Live Oak Publishing Company (which published the *Suwannee Democrat*) during these years.

Hillman was the first person from Florida to enter the celebrated Glidden Tour of 1911, a road rally in which the reliability and endurance of early cars and their drivers were tested. The 1911 tour of sixty-four cars traveled from New York to Jacksonville at a time when most roads were nothing more than dirt trails. Cars often broke down, were damaged in accidents and encountered nearly impassable roads. Drivers had to learn how to fix their cars on the go; many cars never finished the tour. The 1911 race lasted two weeks and covered 1,476 miles, the longest and toughest tour undertaken to that point. The last of its overnight stops was made in Live Oak before finishing in Jacksonville. Years later, Hillman would remember the tour as one of the most pleasant times in his life.

Captain Hillman became Suwannee County's first millionaire (not adjusted for inflation) at a time when the average person's annual salary was between $200 and $400. He and his wife, although childless, were generous with their riches. Hillman was known to give away silver dollars to the first one hundred children who visited him on Christmas Day, and he donated funds for the construction of the Methodist church and preacher's home in Live Oak. He also showed an interest in the school system. Hillman served as a city councilman when Live Oak City Hall (now the headquarters of the Suwannee County Chamber of Commerce) was constructed in 1908–9, and he later served under Live Oak native Governor Cary Hardee as the chairman of the Florida State Road Department (now the Florida Department of Transportation).

Winder Josephus Hillman died on August 29, 1931, and was mourned by the whole county and state. He and his wife (who died in 1943) are buried in the Live Oak Cemetery. His obituary reads, "Fond memories will linger thru out the remainder of the lives of those who were the friends and associates of Captain W.J. Hillman." He was truly a great man who helped not only Suwannee County but also the whole state of Florida.

## THE HILLMAN BRIDGE

Hillman's legacy has lived on in a bridge constructed over the Suwannee River in 1925–26 (and officially dedicated in 1927) named in his honor. The first vehicle bridge at Ellaville (formerly Columbus) had been constructed in 1908, but by the early 1920s, it had outlived its usefulness. The 1920s was a period of heavy migration to Florida, before the Great Depression damaged the nation's economy. As part of this migration, the State of Florida enacted a highway-building spree, including bridges over major waterways.

The State of Florida contracted with the R.H.H. Blackwell Company of East Aurora, New York, to construct a new bridge near the confluence of the Suwannee and Withlacoochee Rivers using federal aid; the bridge cost $150,000 to complete and was of the Pratt metal-truss type. The need for the bridge was obvious, but the naming of the bridge caused a ruckus.

During construction, the bridge was known as the Hillman Bridge, after Captain W.J. Hillman. As part of the Florida State Road Department, he had pushed for funding of the bridge. Shortly before the bridge was completed, some within the Florida Chamber of Commerce decided that

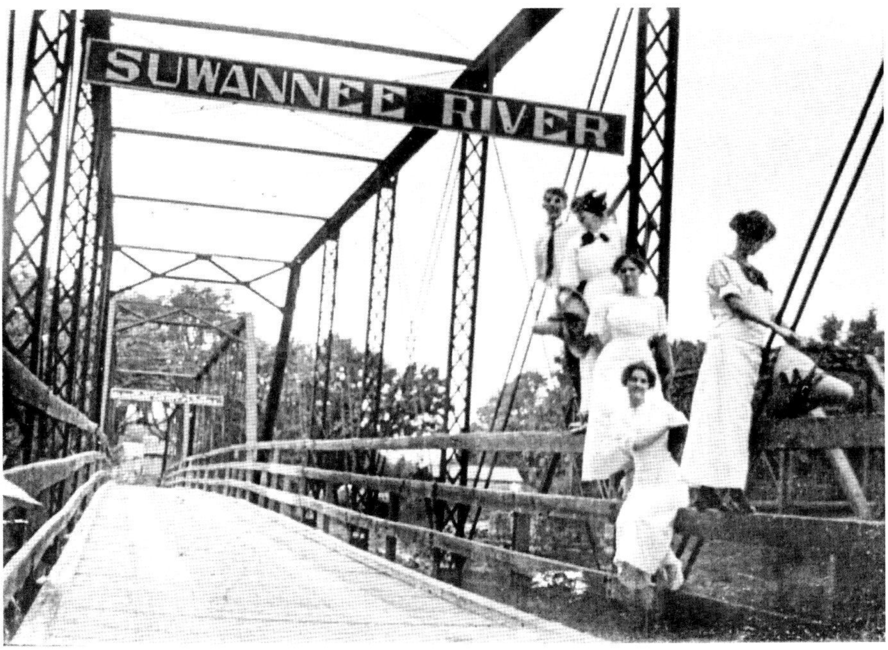


First vehicle bridge at Ellaville, circa 1910. *State Archives of Florida.*

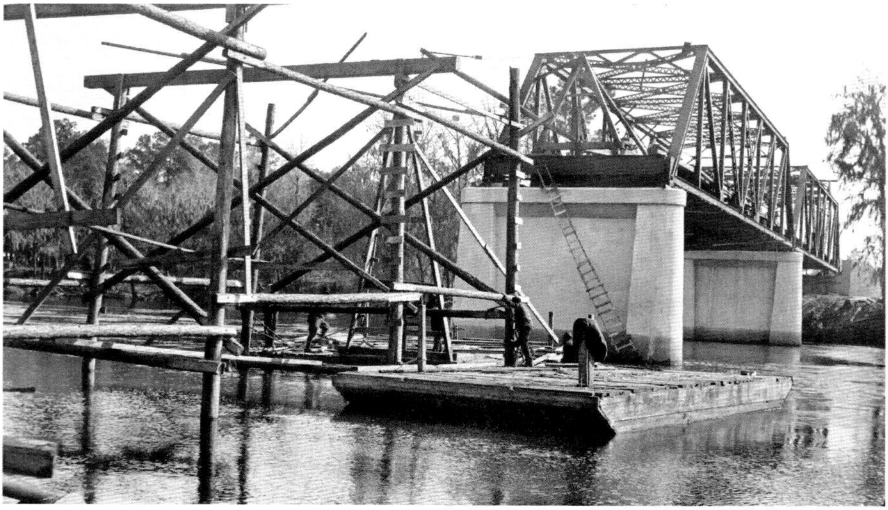

Hillman Bridge under construction, 1926. *State Archives of Florida.*

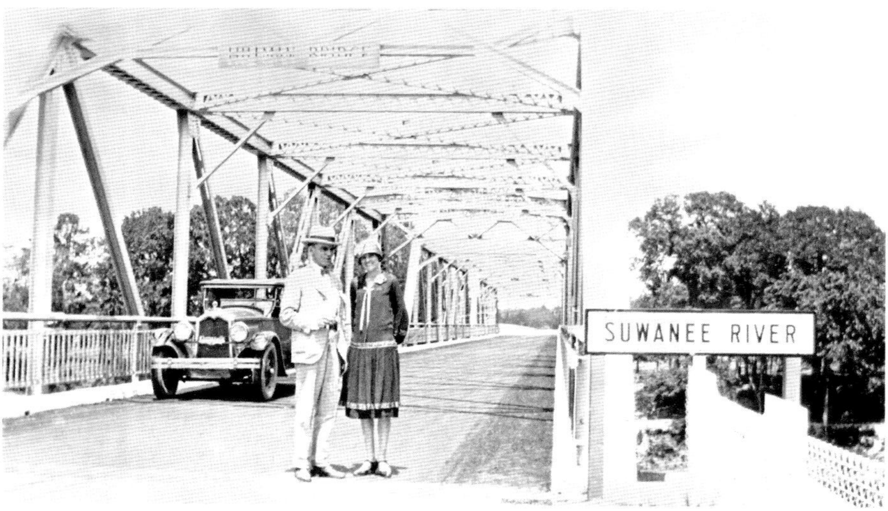


Hillman Bridge shortly after completion, 1927. Note the spelling of the sign to the right of the bridge. *State Archives of Florida.*

naming the bridge after an individual would serve no good purpose and instead proposed naming it after the Suwannee River or Stephen Foster, the songwriter who had made the river famous. The chamber of commerce argued that naming the bridge after Hillman would be as distinctive to the average tourist as "Bridge no. 1313."

The state chamber's questions made headlines as reporters took both sides of the story. However, "Hillman" stuck, and the span was named the Hillman Bridge when it was dedicated in 1927. A prominent sign beside the 910-foot-long bridge reminded tourists that they were crossing the famous "Suwanee" River.

After nearly sixty years, the Hillman Bridge was abandoned in 1983 after a truck carrying a large load struck one of the steel crossbeams, making the bridge unsound for large vehicles. The structure was already on the list of bridges to be replaced, so the state moved up its timetable and completed a new bridge in 1986. The Hillman Bridge still stands as a walking trail across the river within the Suwannee River State Park.

# 10
# LOST LANDMARKS

Suwannee County has seen its fair share of large and influential homes and buildings. Although some still remain to advertise their grandeur to citizens and visitors alike, others have been lost to the ravages of time. These buildings are gone, but they are not forgotten.

## Dexter House

Horace (or sometimes Horatio) Filmore Dexter was the son of pioneer settlers Thomas D. and Mary Ann Dexter. He was born on September 15, 1849, in modern-day Suwannee County. The Dexter family was one of the wealthiest and most influential families to inhabit Suwannee County, from the time of their arrival until the early 1900s.

When Suwannee County was established on December 21, 1858, Thomas and Mary Ann were living on their plantation west of the Pine Grove community. The first federal census of Suwannee County, in 1860, showed that Thomas Dexter was the largest slave owner in the county, with fifty-three slaves. When the Civil War broke out in 1861, Thomas Dexter was a prosperous merchant and plantation owner. Unfortunately, he would not live to see the end of the war. In October 1862, he was horribly burned in a gin house fire on his plantation. He died on October 21.

Horace Dexter inherited his father's business sense, reestablishing the family's finances in the wake of the Civil War. In late 1893 or early

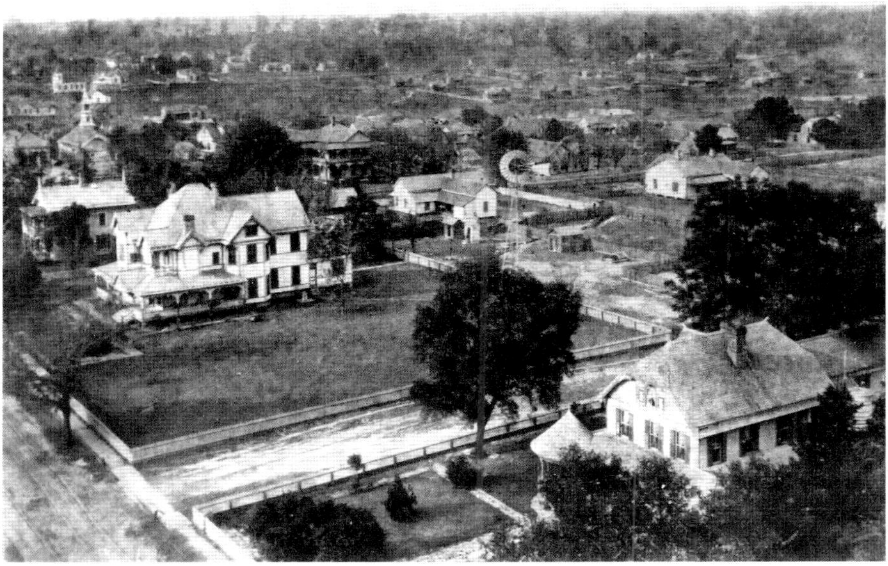

Photograph of Duval Street around 1900; the Dexter home is the large one at center left. *Suwannee County Historical Museum.*

1894, Horace Dexter constructed a large home on Duval Street across from the present Live Oak Fire Department, replacing a more modest frame home already there. The Dexter home was one of the largest (if not the largest) dwellings on Duval Street and in all of Live Oak at the time; tax rolls of the early 1900s show that it was worth more than even Thomas Dowling's stately and slightly newer home one block away. This is even more impressive when one realizes that Horace Dexter built another house next door that was nearly as large and expensive as his own was, and Duval Street at the time was lined with the homes of the wealthiest and most influential citizens of Live Oak and Suwannee County. The imposing residence was a fitting abode for a man who was involved in many local business endeavors, including the construction of part of the present downtown business district, a skating rink and the brick two-story Hotel Bon-Air situated where the chamber of commerce is now located. At Horace Dexter's death in 1907 at the age of fifty-eight, his insurance, stocks, bonds and unpaid loans to various citizens alone had a value of $122,000 (more than $3.1 million in 2015 dollars), apparently not including his homes, businesses and thousands of acres of land throughout the county.

The Dexter home on Duval Street passed to Horace's wife, Lizzie, and others before the City of Live Oak purchased the property for use as a recreation center in 1956. The original intent was to renovate the home for use as a recreation building, but due to its age and condition it was decided to tear down the old home to allow construction of the recreation department building (now John Hale Park), which was completed in 1958.

## SUWANNEE HOTEL

By 1905, Live Oak was the fifth-largest city in Florida. Several railroads crisscrossed the landscape, meeting in the county seat. Visitors from all around the world would travel to Suwannee County to enjoy the natural beauty of the Suwannee River or perhaps tour the manufacturing facilities in town. These visitors needed a place to stay.

Although Live Oak had several hotels and boardinghouses that had been around for twenty or thirty years, there was the need for a modern, opulent hotel that would showcase Live Oak's position as one of the largest cities in the state. A group of twenty-nine businessmen gathered in January 1907 and petitioned the state to incorporate a business to construct a new hotel or hotels. The Suwannee Hotel Company was composed of some of the most influential of Live Oak's men, including W.J. Hillman (president), S.A. Hinely (vice president), B.W. Helvenston (secretary), D.E. Horn (treasurer), Frank Drew and R.L. Dowling. The company began with stock in the amount of $25,000.

The conglomeration moved swiftly and, by 1908, had completed a hotel across the street from the Suwannee County Courthouse, two blocks from the main railroad hub in town. The Suwannee Hotel, also called Hotel Suwannee, was a three-story brick structure with fifty-six rooms (according to a later inventory of hotels conducted by the chamber of commerce). The hotel quickly became the go-to place for railroad and vehicle travelers in Suwannee County.

By 1913, the Suwannee Hotel Company had sold the hotel to L.L. Froneberger. During this period, the hotel was advertised in various

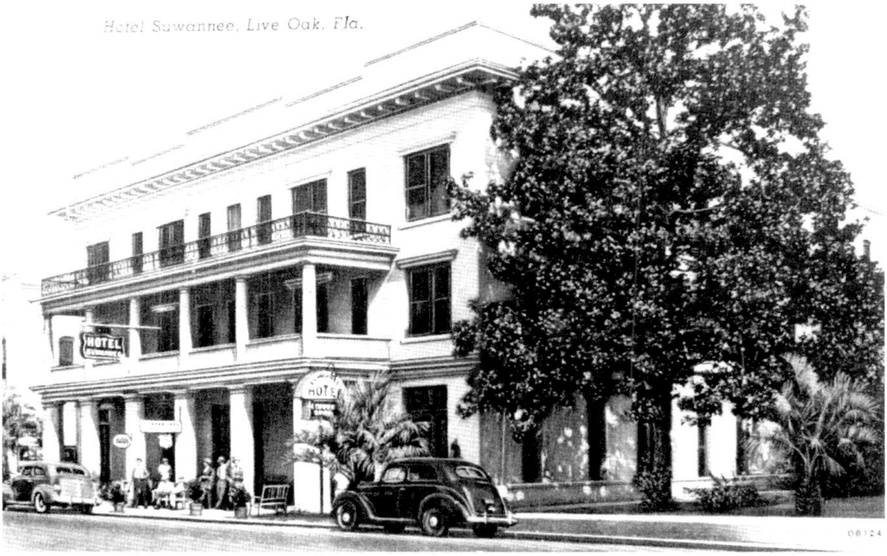


Suwannee Hotel, circa 1945. *State Archives of Florida.*

newspapers and other publications around the country. The April edition of the 1913 *Club Journal* from the Automobile Club of America prominently listed the hotel on several pages, each advertising the steam-heated rooms.

The hotel was owned by J.R. Randle by 1926–27, when it was advertised as the "Headquarters for the Kiwanis, Rotary, and A.B.C. Clubs." The manager was I.F. Williams; the hotel's motto was "Comfort, Service and Courtesy."

According to the *Florida Times-Union* of Jacksonville, in 1928, a new bus line was instituted between Jacksonville and Live Oak, operating in conjunction with the Seaboard Air Line Railway Company. The "palatial parlor buses, modern in every respect with a capacity of thirty passengers with spacious baggage compartments," would make four daily round trips. The buses were named after Confederate generals: Lee, Longstreet, Stewart, Jackson and Beauregard. Their points of arrival in Live Oak were the Suwannee Hotel, the Kalil Drug Store and the Seaboard Air Line Railway Station.

A menu from the same year shows that the Hotel Suwannee Restaurant (under the ownership of J.R. Randle) had a variety of foods. Main courses included smothered spring chicken and breaded veal cutlets in tomato sauce, with pearl grits, buttered potatoes and succotash as side dishes.

The Suwannee Hotel continued to be a fixture in Suwannee County for many years. The restaurant was known by several names as owners

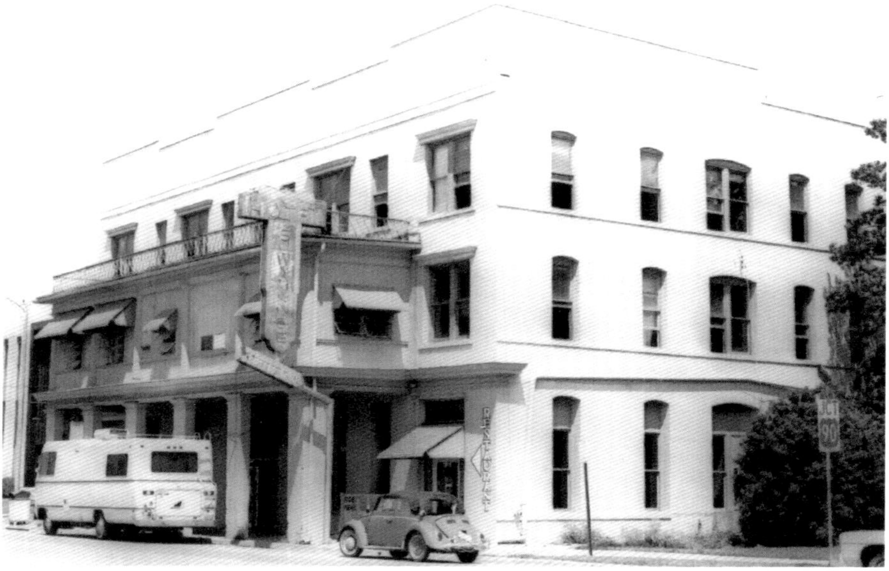


Suwannee Hotel in its waning years, circa 1970. *Suwannee County Historical Museum.*

came and went. Under the management of John Marvin Philips (who also served as mayor for twenty-six years) and his wife, Lillian, it was known as the Suwannee Hotel and Dining Room. Maudine Jackson Glisson, who had previously opened the Mayo Café, was recruited to run the restaurant in the Suwannee Hotel; at the time, it was known as the Suwannee Hotel Coffee Shop.

Eventually, the construction of Interstate 10 on the northern outskirts of Live Oak, coupled with a shift in travelers' tastes, led to the gradual decline of the Suwannee Hotel. By 1974, the Randle Hotel Company, which consisted of one deceased trustee, owned the hotel. A reconstituted Randle Hotel Company, comprising the heirs of the last original trustee, took ownership of the property. However, times had changed, and the old Suwannee Hotel was torn down around 1975 to make way for bank additions.

## PARSHLEY BUILDING

The Parshley family was a prominent part of Suwannee County's history for more than fifty years, and its mark can still be felt. Live Oak especially

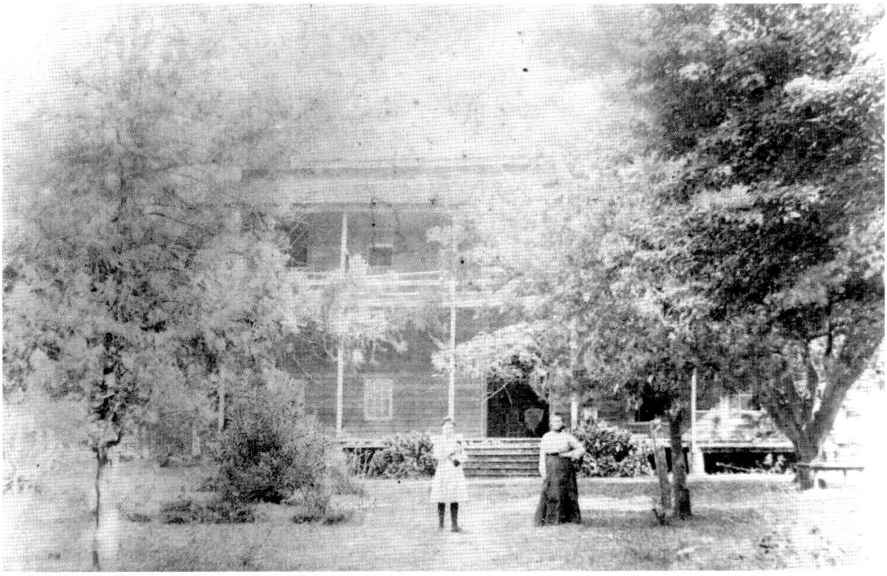

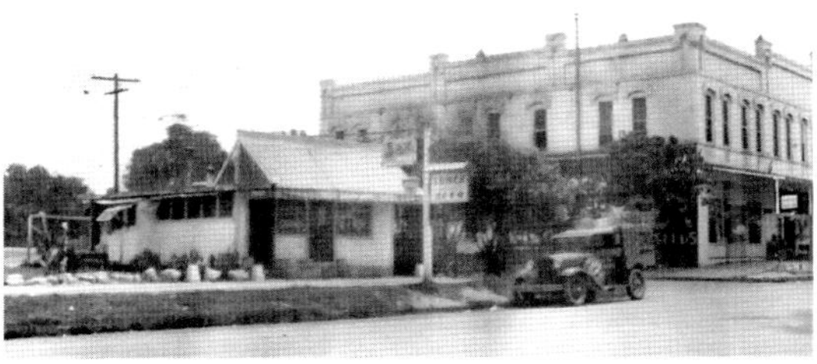

*Above*: Parshley home, circa 1900. *Suwannee County Historical Museum.*

*Left*: Parshley Building (*right*) and nearby structures in June 1925. *Suwannee County Historical Museum.*

reaped benefits from the family; much of the city's success can be directly attributed to the family members.

The Parshley family home had been constructed hurriedly by patriarch John Parshley in 1867 across the street from where the Suwannee County Courthouse would one day be located. The home was large but rather plainly built, a necessity because of the rapidity in which it had been constructed to house the family during the cold winter of 1867. John Parshley died in 1868, but his wife, Nancy, continued her husband's business prospects. She lived in the home until her death in 1897. By 1904, the home had seen better days, and the family decided to tear down the old building, as the area around the house had since become part of the downtown business district.

In the home's place, a large, two-story brick commercial building was constructed in or about 1904 to help with the expanded business prospects that were arriving in Live Oak. The building was aptly named the Parshley Building, after the prominent family. Numerous businesses occupied both floors of the structure.

The Parshley Building's location across from the courthouse made it ideal to accommodate lawyers and court-related functions. It also housed the usual assortment of merchants. Some of the businesses located in the Parshley Building during its lifetime included a bakery, a motion picture theater, electric supply companies, plumbing companies, tailors, general stores, paint stores, doctor's offices, coffee shops, beauty shops and a school of commerce.

Helen Parshley, widow of John and Nancy's son Wilbur, lived in the upstairs portion of the Parshley Building until her death in 1957. In 1964, Hurricane Dora flooded much of the downtown business district, but the Parshley Building remained on dry ground. The First National Bank, whose building at the main intersection of Live Oak had been flooded during Hurricane Dora, decided to build on higher ground. Seeing an opportunity, the bank bought out the Parshley Building and tore it down. The structure was replaced by a two-story bank building in 1966.

These buildings, and many more, are long gone. Their memories linger in various public records and in the minds of those who still recall them.

PART III

# LOST WAYS OF LIFE

11

# EARLY FLORIDA TOURISM, SUWANNEE SPRINGS STYLE

Suwannee Springs has long held a special place in local history. Native Americans and people of European descent had frequented the area since well before Florida became a state. Some were drawn to the area's natural beauty, but many came for the supposed healing powers of the mineral springs. It was not long before perceptive businessmen saw the potential to develop the springs.

The first known American to establish himself at Suwannee Springs was Francis J. Ross, formerly of Jacksonville. In 1831, he purchased the springs and surrounding property from the United States for $5,000 (about $115,000 in 2015 dollars) and began constructing a resort there. By 1835, a Jacksonville newspaper reported that Ross's establishment could hold 150 guests, with the main building having a hall large enough to accommodate 200 people at once. Spring baths and showers allowed the old and infirm to enjoy the healing waters, and stagecoach travel between Tallahassee and Jacksonville allowed weekly access to the springs. However, the Second Seminole War of 1835–42 severely curtailed activities at Suwannee Springs, and a nationwide financial panic in 1837 finally encouraged Ross to sell the resort in 1838.

The end of the Second Seminole War and the addition of ferries and bridges that sprang up at or near Suwannee Springs allowed greater access for visitors. Guesthouses at Suwannee Springs were advertised in regional newspapers as being "the very best fare that can be obtained in this section of the country," and "beds will be properly attended to and kept clean and

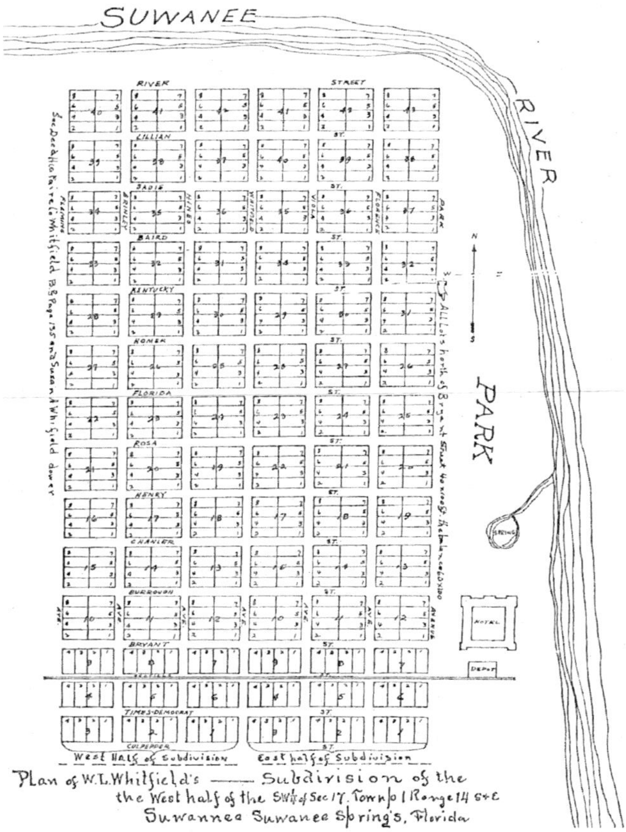


*Left*: W.L. Whitfields's subdivision of Suwannee Springs, circa 1884. Note springs and hotel at bottom right. *Suwannee County Clerk of Court.*

*Below*: The first major hotel at Suwannee Springs, circa 1884. *Suwannee County Clerk of Court.*

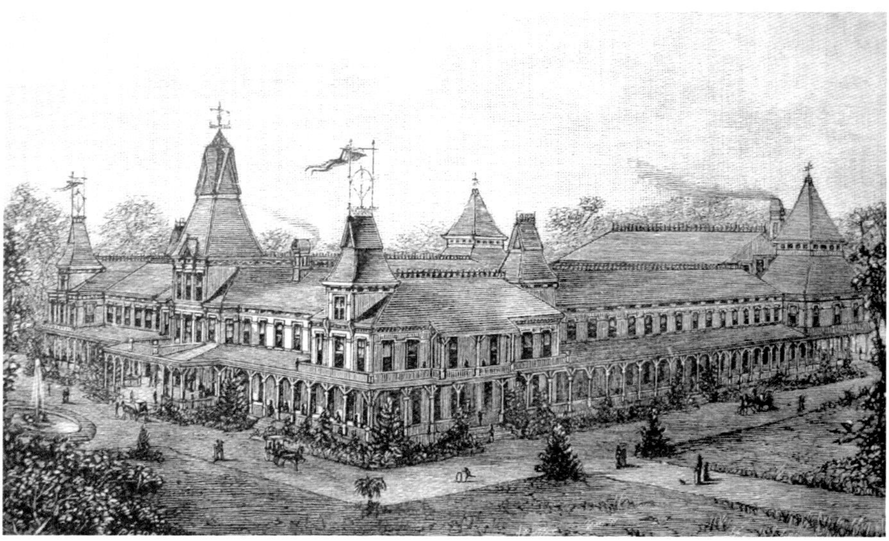

airy." Guests were served such local delicacies as gopher gumbo while they relaxed in the mineral springs or hunted on the vast property.

After the Civil War, the proprietors of Suwannee Springs gradually expanded the resort to include a spacious hotel, a trolley line that ran down to the bathing area, exercise courts, a bowling alley, a water bottling plant and the stone walls around the springs that still exist today. The first major hotel at Suwannee Springs after the Civil War, built by Levi Scoville and Jesse Culpepper, was a massive five-turreted wood structure with 125 rooms and a great open central square.

Unfortunately, the magnificent hotel burned down on January 17, 1884, just after completion. A report in the *New York Times* stated that the building was "probably the finest structure of the kind in the State." Details from the *Times* show that the fire started about four-thirty in the morning on the second floor, above the kitchen, and quickly spread to the rest of the building due to winds. The estimated one hundred guests included a good number of invalids, and most were from the North. All the guests were reported saved, although a few had broken limbs due to having to jump out of their second-story windows. An African American servant girl and boy were reported missing, and it was feared that they were killed in the fire. So traumatic was the loss that a special train was sent from Jacksonville to help in relief efforts for the many displaced guests. The hotel was underinsured, being valued at $95,000 (approximately $2.5 million in 2015 dollars) but with only $51,000 in insurance.

After the destruction of the first hotel, the owners decided that putting all their eggs in one basket had not been the wisest move; a second hotel completed in 1885 had only twenty-five rooms, was built of brick and had numerous cottages around the premises so that the entire guest capacity would not be lost in one fire. The hotel and its outbuildings were advertised in numerous newspapers around the United States, touting the healing waters of Suwannee Springs.

In conjunction with the second hotel, a railroad station was built at nearby Suwannee Station. This station, about two miles from Suwannee Springs, was fashioned out of the same native stones that formed part of the Suwannee Springs enclosure. A horse-drawn tram carried passengers from the railroad station to the springs, where they would indulge themselves in some of the various activities of the health resort.

The Suwannee Springs property had a variety of owners over the years. In 1893, the Suwannee Springs Company was established by Andrew Hanley, John D. Robinson Jr. and Tyre J. Dinkins with capital of $100,000. The

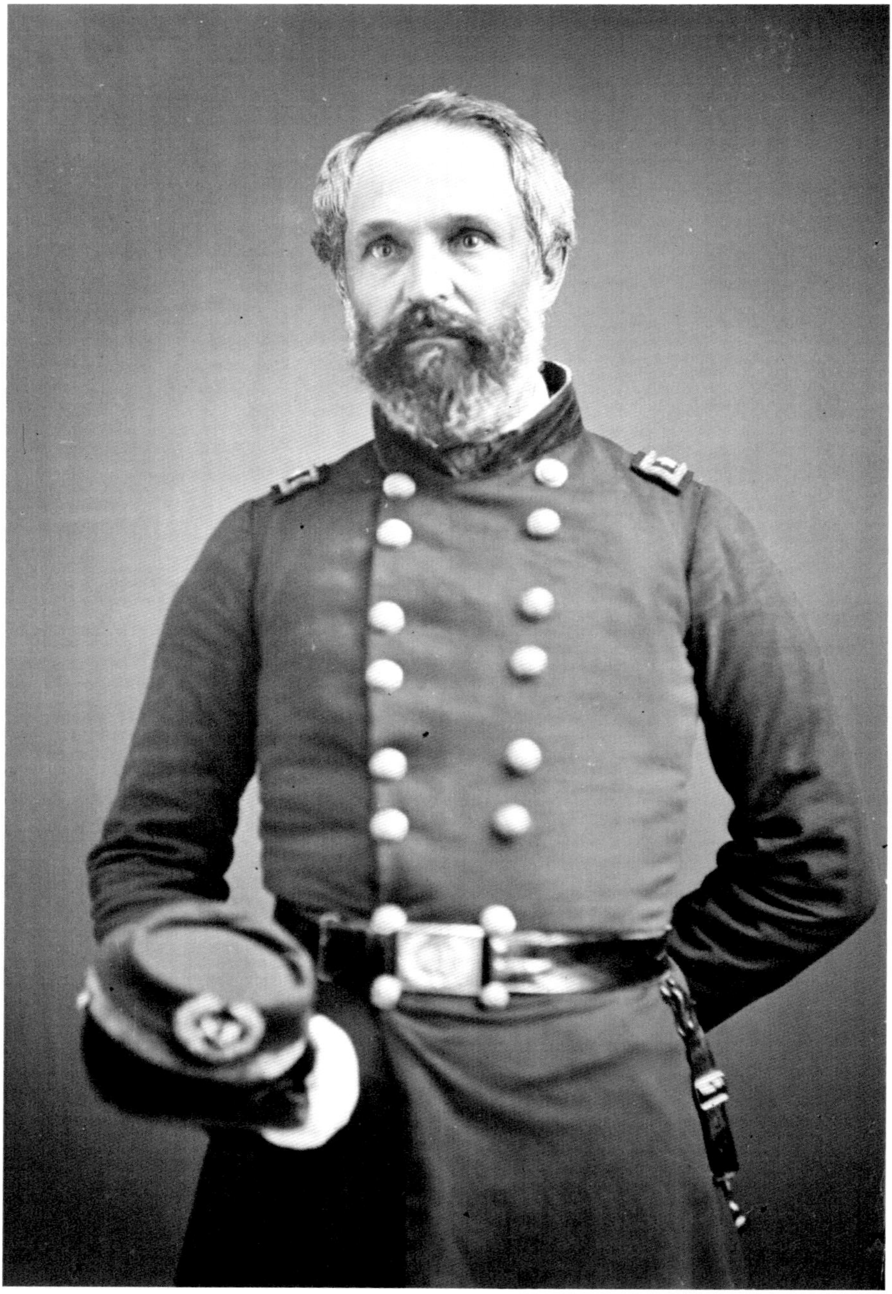

Union brigadier general Robert Bruce Van Valkenburgh, one of the thousands of post–Civil War visitors to Suwannee Springs in the late 1800s. He died there on August 1, 1888. *FindAGrave.com.*

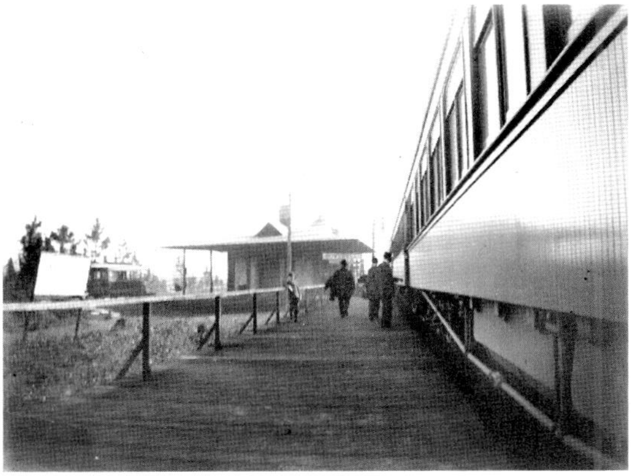

*Left*: Suwannee Station, late 1800s. Note the horse-drawn tram in left background. *Columbia County Chamber of Commerce.*

*Below*: Abandoned cottages at Suwannee Springs, 1974. *State Archives of Florida.*

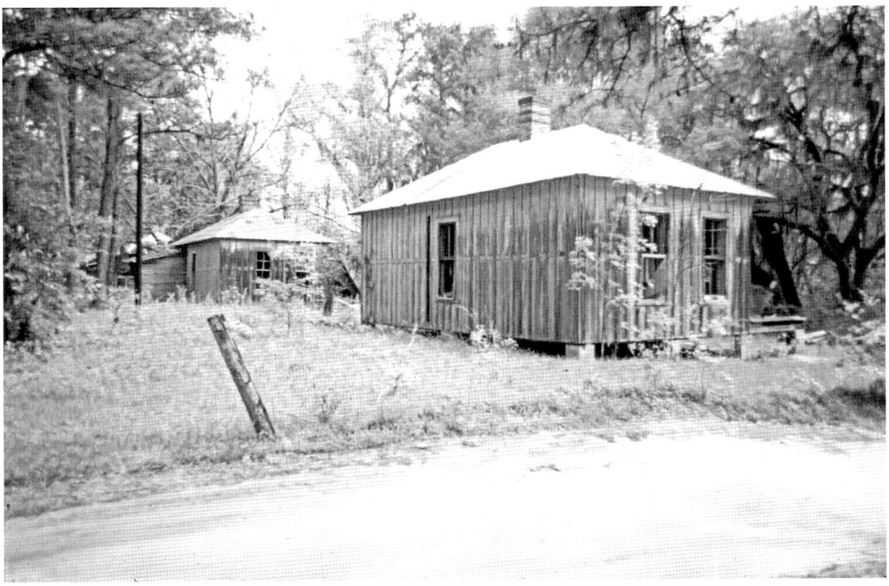

purposes included operating a hotel; bottling, barreling and shipping mineral water; and establishing a sanitarium. In late 1904, the Suwannee Sulphur Springs Company was established by C.J. McGehee, B.W. Helvenston, F.L. Rees, C.D. Blackwell and C.B. Davis. The purpose of this successor company was to develop and improve

> *the Suwannee Sulphur Springs property, the sale of water from the Spring, the erection and maintenance of bath-houses, pavilions, residences, cottages and hotels for the guests and ownership with right to sell off such lands as*

> *shall be necessary to the proper handling of said property, and to further the interest thereof as pleasure and health resort.*

Unfortunately, the second hotel burned down in November 1901; however, the owners did not lose the eighteen surrounding cottages or the hotel annex, which was more than one hundred feet away. The second hotel's annex then became the third hotel, with the cottages continuing to receive guests through the first decades of the twentieth century.

As scientific evidence began to show that sulfur did not hold miraculous healing powers, the visitors became fewer and fewer, and the community of Suwannee Springs eventually dried up. Fire finally destroyed the third hotel in 1925; most of the guest cabins have since vanished.

Over the years, the property was purchased by a variety of individuals who wished to reclaim some of the springs' glory days. However, repeated discussions about rebuilding a hotel and cabins have met with little commercial interest, and the site is now a local park. Visitors can still walk some of the same trails that their ancestors walked nearly two hundred years ago. The ruins of the third hotel and several cabins hint at the commercial success of Suwannee Springs in prior years.

12

# GHOST TOWN

## *Columbus*

Changes in travel modes, the location of natural resources and a variety of other events have shifted the population centers of Suwannee County over the years. As a result, many once-thriving communities no longer exist or are a shadow of their former selves. Such is the case with the once-flourishing town of Columbus.

Columbus was one of the earliest chartered American communities in Suwannee County. In 1833, the Florida legislature authorized Paul M'Cormic (McCormick) to establish a ferry at the confluence of the Suwannee and Withlacoochee Rivers for five years. Six years later, on February 8, 1839, David Platt was authorized to build a ferry or toll bridge at the same location. The population quickly mushroomed, as there were enough people in the locale for a post office named Columbus to be established there on February 17, 1842. A stagecoach road eventually joined Columbus on the western boundary with Suwannee (Lower Mineral) Springs and beyond; County Road 132 roughly follows part of this old road, and it is still commonly known as the Stagecoach Road. A visitor to Columbus, writing in the *St. Augustine News* in late 1843, described the community as having two large stores (with others under construction) and other mercantile establishments that bought cotton from surrounding counties. The same visitor stated that over three thousand bales of cotton were shipped in the fall of 1843 from Columbus, with towering piles of cotton still awaiting shipment on the riverbanks. Columbus's population was already some five hundred people at that time. On March 14, 1844, the governor submitted a request to establish a mail route from Cedar Key to Columbus, intersecting the central line from Tallahassee to Jacksonville. The governor stated that the road

> *would be of great importance to the citizens of Madison, Alachua, Columbia, and Hamilton, Florida, there being no communication by mail between those places: and whereas, as that portion of the country bordering on the Suwannee River is being settled by an enterprizing* [sic] *and industrious community, the products of whose industry is every year increasing.*

In recognition of the community's growth, on the same date, March 14, 1844, the town of Columbus was incorporated, with John W.C. Loud, David Platt and George H. Smith superintending until elections could be held. The following day, Joseph B. Watts, Francis Jones, David Platt, Enoch Hall, A. Vann, Loud and Sandler formed a company to establish a toll bridge at Columbus; their charter would be good for ten years. The following year, the Florida legislature requested that the federal government provide $8,000 to open a mail route to be operated from Columbus to Garey's Ferry (now Middleburg in Clay County). The year 1845 also saw the first known steamboat with a regular run on the Suwannee River, *Orpheus,* carrying the weekly mail between Cedar Key and Columbus. Repeated attempts to clear obstructions along the Suwannee River at least to Columbus met with little success, as the issue was brought up almost annually until the eve of the Civil War.

Columbus was large enough in 1847 and again in 1853 to be one of Columbia County's election precincts (Suwannee County did not yet exist). An indication of the town's size and commerce can be gauged by the governor's authorization in 1849 to reimburse twelve dollars to Mary A. Hardee and a Mrs. Burnett for the taverns that each kept in Columbus. In January 1855, the charter of the Columbus Bridge Company was renewed for another ten years; it was probably the name of the company that had been created by legislative action in 1844. By the following year, however, the Columbus Bridge Company had apparently gone out of business, because William H. Watson was authorized to operate ferries at Columbus to both Hamilton and Madison Counties for a period of ten years.

## Columbus during the Civil War

Despite the apparently unsuccessful attempts to totally clear the Suwannee River of obstructions, Columbus was still important enough during the Civil War to have the only completed railroad bridge across the Suwannee River. The Pensacola & Georgia Railroad had completed this bridge in early 1861, just before the beginning of the war. An interesting fact about the bridge was that it was a wood, covered bridge, and after each train went through it, workers had to rush onto the bridge to put out any embers from the engine's smokestack so that the entire bridge did not catch fire. This bridge served as the primary supply line for Confederate forces outside of Florida, and it became all the more important after 1863, when the fall of Vicksburg cut off Confederate supplies from Arkansas and Texas. In 1864, Union troops were ordered to march from Jacksonville and destroy the bridge at Columbus. Brigadier General Joseph Finnegan, commanding Confederate forces in the area, was concerned that the Union forces would outflank him and attack

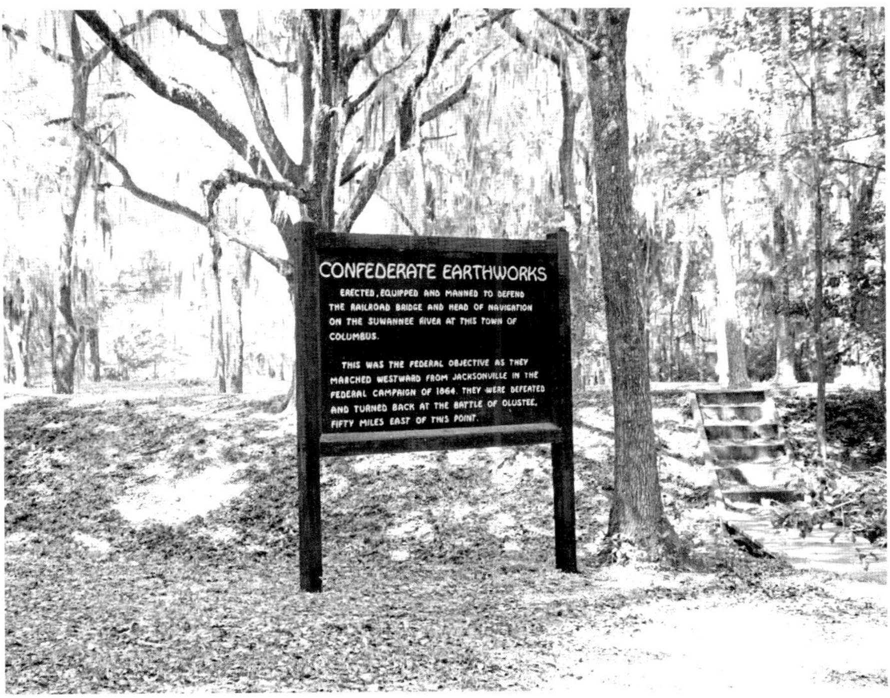


Earthworks at Suwannee River State Park, circa 1950. *State Archives of Florida.*

the railroad bridge on the Suwannee River, where he had only thirty men stationed. Union forces were defeated at the Battle of Olustee, east of Lake City, on February 20, 1864, by Confederate forces under Finnegan. The bridge over the Suwannee River at Columbus thus remained in Confederate hands, supplying Confederate forces until the end of the war. Confederate troops were regularly stationed at the vital railroad junction until the end of the war. Confederate earthworks built near the bridge as a final defensive position remain visible and are part of Suwannee River State Park.

## THE END OF COLUMBUS

With the end of the Civil War in 1865, George Franklin Drew moved to the Columbus area and built a sawmill near his home across the Suwannee River in Madison County; this had the effect of drawing people and businesses to the Madison County side of the river. In 1868, the Suwannee Steamboat Company was chartered with a goal of transferring freight and produce between Clay's Landing and the town of Columbus in Suwannee County. The charter gave sole navigation rights between those two points to the Suwannee Steamboat Company, and any person or persons navigating

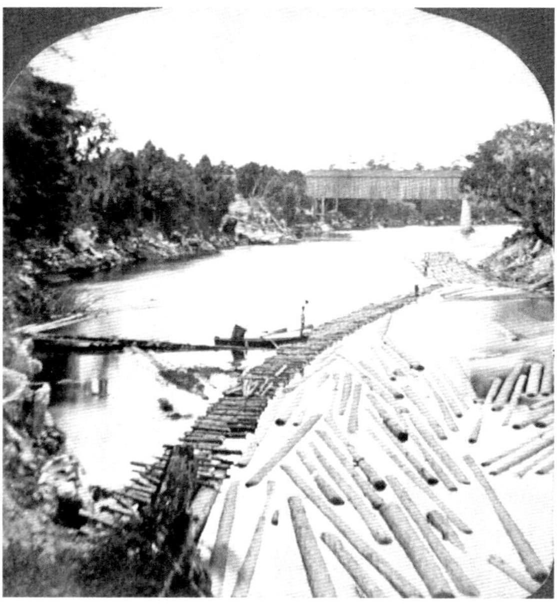

Log boom on the Suwannee River at Columbus (Ellaville), circa 1870s. The railroad bridge is in the background. *State Archives of Florida.*

or transporting freights or produce without permission of the Suwannee Steamboat Company would be guilty of a misdemeanor and fined between $200 and $500. The charter was approved on August 3, 1868, and was good for twenty years unless the steamboat company failed to perform the duties within five years. Columbus was still a large enough community in 1869 that it was one of Suwannee County's six polling places to determine the county seat. During this time, Charles Dean ran the ferry crossing among Suwannee, Hamilton and Madison Counties; his home overlooked the ferry and the Suwannee River on the Suwannee County side.

By 1873, Columbus had dried up as markets shifted and financial depression hit the United States. The post office had been renamed Ellaville in 1872 and moved to the Madison County side of the river; it eventually returned to the Suwannee County side before closing for good in 1943. All that remains of Columbus today are a cemetery, Confederate earthworks from the Civil War, the remains of the original ferry landing and a few ghostly ruins. These are all found within Suwannee River State Park.

# 13

# STEAMBOATING ON THE SUWANNEE

The popularity of the Suwannee River did not begin with Stephen Foster's song "Old Folks at Home" (better known as "Way Down Upon the Swanee River"), but it did romanticize the river for those who had never seen it. As a result, thousands visited Florida to see the famed "Swanee" River; one of the best ways to do so was to take a steamboat cruise down the famous river.

## Pre–Civil War Steamboats

Steamboats plied the Suwannee River for nearly a century, churning the dark waters between the mid-1830s and early 1920s. The first known steamboat to enter the Suwannee River was *Minerva,* which served the federal government along with several other steamboats at the mouth of the Suwannee River in 1836. The sudden interest in the Suwannee River was due to the instigation of the Second Seminole War in late December 1835, a war that would rage until 1842. Steamboats that could steam upriver to what is now Suwannee River State Park and beyond supplied several outposts during the Second Seminole War, as there were few major roads and the scattered trails were hazardous due to Seminole raids. Another steamboat, the government-owned *Izard,* ran aground in the Withlacoochee River after leaving the Suwannee River about the same time *Minerva* was operating.

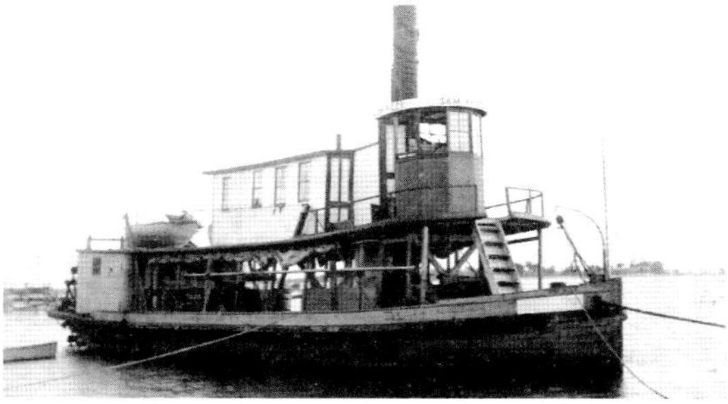

Steamboat *Sam Pyles* off Cedar Key, circa 1900. *State Archives of Florida.*

According to some local sources, steamboats were used in 1839 to provide supplies to the army outpost at or near Suwannee Springs. The post had been cut off from supplies due to floodwaters and was crowded with settlers escaping Seminole attacks.

Due to various hazards, a proposal (the first of many) was made in 1839 to clear the oyster bars at the Suwannee River's mouth and to eliminate any obstructions in the lower part of the river. A nine-foot-deep channel was also recommended to allow larger steamboats to safely navigate the dark river. Some work was apparently done on the Suwannee River by 1845, when the first commercial steamboat, *Orpheus*, began sailing up the Suwannee River according to an October 25 article in the *St. Augustine News*. According to the article, *Orpheus* was built in New Orleans and was

> *a most beautiful vessel, 136 feet in length, and is fitted up in fine style with 18 staterooms. She will carry the U.S. Mail from Cedar Keys to the new town of Santa Fe on the Santa Fe River, in Columbia County, once a week and will also run up the Suwannee to the flourishing town of Columbus.*

Unfortunately, *Orpheus* was lost on the Suwannee River sometime in 1847, when a newspaper article advertised an auction for its remains where they lay.

Another steamboat to operate on the Suwannee River was the forty-nine-ton, one-deck *Glasgow*, between 1849 and 1851, and possibly even longer. It was one hundred feet long, nineteen feet wide and less than three feet deep, making it suitable for the shallow reaches in the Suwannee River. Its master and part-time owner was David Bell. Unfortunately, like some of the other steamboats mentioned in this chapter, there are no known photographs of *Glasgow* while it was in service.

## Madison

In 1854 or 1855, Captain James Tucker, a native of Kentucky, brought the steamboat *Madison* to the Suwannee River from where it was constructed in New Albany, Indiana. *Madison* was listed at ninety-nine tons and was 120 feet long, 22 feet wide and 4 feet deep and was named for the town of Madison, where Captain Tucker lived. Despite its future fame, there are no known photographs of *Madison* while it was in service. *Madison*'s first owner in Florida was Mr. E. Richards of Cedar Key, and its first master was W.P. Pegman (or Pigman), who was Captain Tucker's partner. Tucker eventually was awarded a twice-a-month mail service between Columbus (now Suwannee River State Park) and the town of Bayport (Hernando County) on the Gulf of Mexico. This mail route connected at Cedar Key, which at the time was a center of activity between New Orleans and Key West. *Madison* also served as a floating general store, trading merchandise for the settlers' venison, hams, hides, tallow, honey, chickens, eggs and whatever else they could barter. Its whistle could be heard ten miles away, giving everyone time to travel to the steamboat landing. *Madison* would remain at a landing until everyone was done trading and then move on to the next one.

In 1859, Captain Tucker brought another steamboat, *Colonel Cottrell*, into the Suwannee River. This steamboat was probably named for a prominent family of the time who lived at Old Town along the Suwannee River. By 1860, Tucker had transferred the operations of *Madison* to his cousin C.C. Young and moved to the Fernandina area to live off the income from his mail contracts. Before that time, however, Tucker and *Madison* had proven that the Suwannee River was navigable all the way up to White Springs (courtesy of heavy rain and flooding), despite the loss of *Madison*'s pilothouse and funnels to the overhanging trees.

The beginning of the Civil War gave *Madison* another means of service; it would help to protect Confederate interests on the Suwannee River and also attack Federal forces stationed at Cedar Key. The U.S. government, in a move to strangle the Confederacy, established a blockade around the coastline from Texas to Virginia, cutting off much-needed foreign supplies. Only fast blockade runners and river-going steamers could use the various inland waterways around the Confederacy, and the Suwannee River was one such location for these activities. Federal supply ships would also deliver goods to the Federal base at Cedar Key (captured at the beginning of the war); this created opportunities for enterprising sailors in the area. A period dispatch states that on July 4, 1861, two companies of the Second Florida

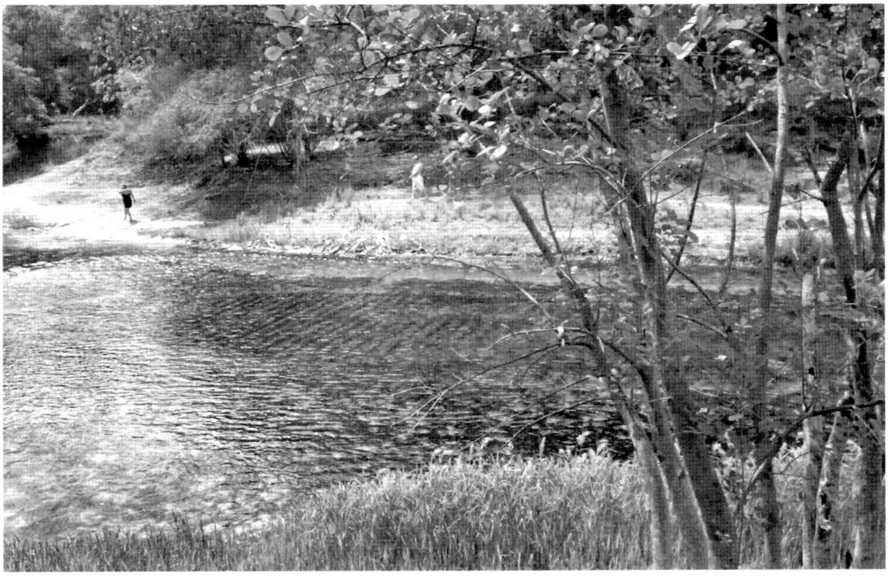

Remains of the steamboat *Madison* in Troy Springs, 2007. *Author's collection.*

Infantry Regiment took *Madison* and captured three schooners loaded with railroad irons, a valuable commodity to the industry-poor South, outside the mouth of the Suwannee River near Cedar Key. *Madison* protected the lower reaches of the Suwannee River for the first half of the Civil War. However, the tide of war turned against the Confederacy, and in September 1863, Captain Tucker ordered *Madison* scuttled in Troy Spring to prevent its capture by the Union, but with the intention of raising it after the war. Citizens in the Troy area (then the county seat of Lafayette County) begged Tucker to first transport a load of corn, but as Tucker was traveling to Virginia, he turned *Madison* over to them to move the corn from Old Town to Troy. Once its last mission was complete, E.J. Davis, John M. Caldwell and Joab Ward ran *Madison* into Troy Spring around 2:00 p.m., pulled out its plugs and watched until it rested on the bottom of the springs.

Unfortunately for Captain Tucker, *Madison* would not remain untouched during the remainder of the war. Its boilers and funnels were cut apart and used to harvest salt and sugar; its cabins and wood above decks were taken for construction materials. By 1865, nothing was left of the once-graceful steamboat except for its sunken hull. Most scholars agree that it is *Madison*'s remains that lie in Troy Spring to this day, where they can be easily seen when the Suwannee River is low.

## Post–Civil War Recovery

The Federal blockade of the Confederacy strangled seagoing commerce, and by the end of the Civil War, steamboating had come to a complete standstill on the Suwannee River, as it had for most waterways in the Confederacy. Several attempts just after the war to revitalize steamboat traffic on the Suwannee River failed, as too many people were recovering from the changes brought about by the end of the war. Gradually, however, enterprising men realized the importance of the Suwannee River to area trade.

On August 3, 1868, the Suwannee Steamboat Company was chartered by Washington Rogers, George W. Rogers, Peter Moran and John A. Boyd of Florida. The company's stated purpose was to transport freight and produce between Cedar Key and Columbus, with exclusive privilege of navigating the Suwannee River above Clay Landing to Columbus. At the time, Columbus was a bustling community where Suwannee River State Park is now located. Despite the destruction brought about by Federal ships and troops during the Civil War, Cedar Key had quickly recovered and was soon home to several large pencil factories that harvested the abundant cedar trees growing around the lower Suwannee River. These factories necessitated transportation of raw goods and supplies to markets throughout the state and country, and the closet railroad for interstate travel was in Suwannee County.

Despite the chartering of the Suwannee Steamboat Company in 1868, it was not until 1872 that the first known postwar steamboat began sailing on the Suwannee River. This steamboat was *Wawenock*, a nearly decade-old vessel built in Maine and used by the U.S. government during the war. Originally some 103 tons and with dimensions of 109 feet by 19 feet by 4.5 feet, it operated out of Norfolk, Virginia, from 1865 to 1868. In 1868, it was reconstructed and emerged from the docks at 128 tons and with dimensions of 118 feet by 27 feet by 5 feet. After a stint in Charleston, South Carolina, by 1872, it was running up the Suwannee River from Cedar Key to New Troy. Once a week, it would connect at Cedar Key with the numerous vessels moving between Key West and New Orleans. In the late summer of 1874, *Wawenock* moved to Pensacola and then beyond before being broken up in 1880. While on the Suwannee River, its captain and master was John Gleason.

After *Wawenock* moved to Pensacola, another steamboat, *David L. Yulee*, was built in Cedar Key and began operations on the Suwannee River. *Yulee* was a plainly built steamboat, with one deck, displacing 89 tons and measuring 82 feet by 22 feet by 4 feet. Most, if not all, of its life was spent on the Suwannee River carrying mainly freight. Its owner and master for most of its life was Samuel C. Reddick, a well-known steamboat captain of the time. *Yulee* served until 1885, when its owners abandoned it near the mouth of the Suwannee River (at what aptly came to be called Yulee's Bend). Its remains rest in the dark waters today.

Another steamboat, the two-decked *Erie*, soon joined *David L. Yulee* plying the Suwannee River. *Erie* was built in Jacksonville in 1876 and displaced a mere 34 tons. It was 70 feet long, 21 feet wide and had a draft of just over 4 feet. Its crew consisted of three officers and twelve men, and it probably carried passengers from time to time, although its normal haul was a variety of goods. *Erie* moved to Cedar Key in the summer of 1880 and was partially owned by merchants along the Suwannee River. In 1883, it was sold to merchants in Manatee County and had left the Suwannee River by 1884.

## HENRY B. PLANT

As railroads expanded throughout Florida in the 1870s and 1880s, they encountered the already existing steamboat lines. At first, it appeared that the railroads would be a complement to steamboats, but time was to tell a different story. Many businessmen chose one method of travel or the other and invested heavily, but Henry Bradley Plant was one man who excelled at both. Plant's company would play a significant role in Suwannee River steamboating (and railroad) history until his death in 1899.

The first steamboat on the Suwannee River brought in by Henry Plant was *Caddo Belle*, which began operations in July 1883. It was built in 1880 in Ohio and displaced 167 tons, measuring 125 feet by 25 feet by 3.5 feet; records of the day list it as being a stern-wheeled two-decker. Like many steamboats of the era, *Caddo Belle* would haul freight on its lower deck and passengers on the upper deck. Advertisements stated that it connected with the newly built railroad in Branford. Unfortunately, *Caddo Belle* was not successful on the Suwannee River. In April 1884, the *Daily Enquirer and Sun* of Columbus, Georgia, reported that it was likely that *Caddo Belle* would be moved to Columbus to replace a steamboat that had been destroyed by fire on the Apalachicola River, at least until a new steamboat was built.

This move apparently happened shortly thereafter, as by the fall of 1885, *Caddo Belle* was abandoned on the Apalachicola River as being unfit for service. Although *Caddo Belle* served as an inauspicious start (its captain had committed suicide in 1881), Plant's steamboats would have better luck in the succeeding years.

While Henry Plant was running the first of several steamboats on the Suwannee River, others were profiting from the route as well. It is very likely that the steamboat *Eva* was used on the Suwannee River starting in November 1881. It displaced 115 tons and was 100 by 22 by 3.5 feet in size. Built in New Orleans in 1875 and owned by interests in Tampa, it was plainly built but listed as having some type of enclosure on its upper deck. The captain during its time on the Suwannee River was Samuel Reddick, the man who had owned *David L. Yulee* during much of its existence. *Eva* served until April 1883, when it was wrecked.

One of the more famous steamboats to travel on the Suwannee River was *Bertha Lee*, built on the Ohio River in 1879. It displaced 121 tons and measured 130 by 21 by 3.8 feet. *Bertha Lee* was transferred to Fort Myers in 1883 after a trip down the Ohio and Mississippi Rivers and then across the Gulf of Mexico. Its owners' intended purpose once reaching Florida was to sail on the Kissimmee River and the connecting lakes from Kissimmee to Lake Okeechobee. One of the great steamboat stories in Florida details *Bertha Lee*'s voyage from Fort Myers to Kissimmee. The trip normally took three to five days, but it took *Bertha Lee* and its crew fifty-three days due to the lack of water depth and its size; at times, the crew had to dig their own channels or wash the dirt away with the steamboat's stern wheel to proceed. Running low on food and wood, the crew took to bartering with Seminole Indians in the area for the necessary supplies.

*Bertha Lee*'s owners quickly realized that it was too large for the Kissimmee River, and after a brief stint on the St. Johns River, it was sold to Captain Benjamin Franklin Hall Jr., who had commanded the vessel during the epic trip from Fort Myers to Kissimmee. Captain Hall brought *Bertha Lee* to the Suwannee River in late 1885 or early 1886. Its exact amount of time on the Suwannee River is unknown, but it was long enough for the boat to be identified with the river in advertisements. *Bertha Lee* eventually moved to the more profitable Apalachicola-Chattahoochee River run but ran aground and was wrecked just after Captain Hall had spent his life savings ($10,000 at the time) on a refit and repairs. After working as a hotel night clerk in Kissimmee, he regained his fortune and purchased several small steamboats for use in central Florida.

By the mid- to late 1880s, several steamboats were plying the Suwannee River, their various owners making a living transporting goods and passengers on the dark waters. Probably the most prominent of the steamboat operators on the Suwannee River during this period was Robert Absalom Ivey of Branford.

## ROBERT A. IVEY

A discussion of steamboating on the Suwannee River would not be complete without mentioning the work of Robert Absalom Ivey. "Captain Bob," as he was known, was the most prolific steamboat builder on the Suwannee River and did much to bring tourism to the area in the 1880s and 1890s. The town of Branford especially benefited from his pursuits; Ivey gave the town its name in honor of his good friend Henry Plant's hometown in Connecticut.

As far as historians can tell, Captain Ivey's first venture in steamboating was *Suwanee* (spelled with one "n"), showing up in records from July 1889 with a length of 70 feet, width of 16.5 feet and draught of 4 feet. There is much confusion as to whether *Suwanee* was a new steamboat built in Branford (probably in 1888) using the engines from an earlier wrecked steamboat by the name of *Susie B.* (constructed in Ohio around 1880), or whether it was *Susie B.* itself that had in the meantime transferred to the Suwannee River and been renamed. Either way, *Suwanee* was sold in September 1889 to interests farther south. Among those who chartered its services over the years was Thomas Edison, the famous inventor who became very fond of the steamboat. Unfortunately, *Suwanee* sank near Moore Haven on Lake Okeechobee during the Great Miami Hurricane of 1926. However, by 1929, Henry Ford, the automobile genius and close friend of Edison, salvaged the engines and some timbers from *Suwanee* and other steamboats for use in a "new" steamboat built for his Greenfield Village and Henry Ford Museum in Dearborn, Michigan. The new vessel was appropriately named *Suwanee*. After sixty-five years of carrying visitors in a shallow lagoon around Greenfield Village, *Suwanee* was permanently docked in 2004 and scrapped in 2011.

Captain Ivey next built a dredge for the U.S. Army Corps of Engineers in 1889 that he also named *Suwanee* (again with one "n"). This *Suwanee* was one hundred feet long, twenty-four feet wide and had a draught of four or five feet, depending on the source. It was an ugly scow-hulled vessel that was first used to clear snags and dredge in the Suwannee River using equipment on its bow. Based on several U.S. Army Chief of Engineers reports, it eventually was used for work on the Ocklawaha River and many other water projects (mainly in southwest Florida) until May 1911, when it was sold to the Hillsborough Dredging Company of Tampa. *Suwanee*'s name was changed to *Dredge Hester*, but it only lasted until July 23, 1911, when it burned in Tampa Bay. Its machinery was salvaged, and the wreck had been dynamited and removed by March 8, 1912.

Captain Ivey next built *Belle of Suwannee*, probably the most famous steamboat to travel on the Suwannee River. It entered service in December 1889. Like Ivey's previous steamboats, *Belle of Suwannee* was built in Branford near where the old railroad depot now stands. *Belle of Suwannee* was constructed like many two-decked stern-wheeled steamboats of its day, displaced 180 tons and was 111 by 24 by 4 feet in size. Captain Ivey named this steamboat after his daughter Bertha, the "belle" in his eyes and the only daughter of his first wife. Bertha was a longtime Branford resident and would marry F.H. George, future judge and mayor of Branford. *Belle of*

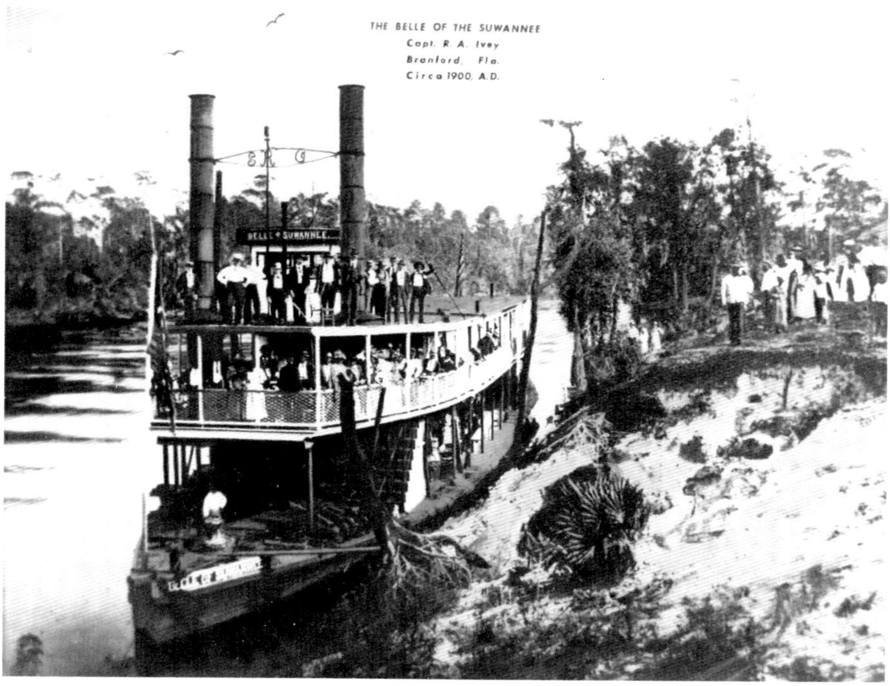


*Belle of Suwannee* at Branford, circa 1895. *State Archives of Florida.*

*Suwannee* was well known in its time, much of it due to its famous bridal suite that was a highlight of Florida honeymoons in the 1890s. The steamboat's Suwannee River catfish dinners were also legendary.

When it was not transporting honeymooners and other passengers, *Belle of Suwannee* transported freight along the Suwannee River. Among the more interesting cargoes it carried was blocks of ice sent from New England to Cedar Key packed in sawdust (used as insulation), from whence it was transported by *Belle* and other steamboats to Dr. Perry McIntosh's icehouse at Luraville. *Belle*'s crew usually numbered fifteen. Its most famous pilot was Dan McQueen, a mulatto who had spent much of his life on the Suwannee River. It is said that McQueen knew every nook and cranny along the Suwannee and could navigate a steamboat in the dark. McQueen had helped to build *Belle of Suwannee* in 1889 and served aboard many steamboats over the years. When he was not piloting steamboats or serving as their master, he taught at an African American school in Old Town.

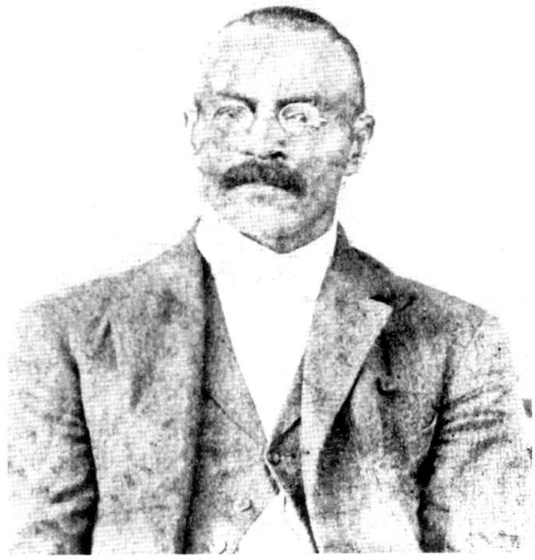

Dan McQueen, riverboat pilot on the Suwannee River, late 1800s. *State Archives of Florida.*

*Belle of Suwannee* steamed on the Suwannee River without incident until the hurricane of 1896 wrecked the economy of the area and caused many casualties. *Belle of Suwannee* was feared lost until Dan McQueen piloted it back to Cedar Key despite the loss of its funnels and pilothouse. After the mass destruction caused by the 1896 hurricane, Captain Ivey sold *Belle of Suwannee* to Captain E.L. Magruder, who also owned other steamboats on the Suwannee River. *Belle* continued to serve in and around the Suwannee River until July 6, 1900, when it sank near Horseshoe Bay, twenty-five miles north of the mouth of the Suwannee River, while towing rafts to Cedar Key.

## Steamboating Heyday

Despite his fame, Captain Ivey was not the only Suwannee River operator of steamboats in the 1880s and 1890s. The years until the end of 1896 would see a variety of individual owners and consortiums running steamboats along the scenic Suwannee River for both business and entertainment purposes. Part of the increased traffic was due to dredging operations carried out by boats such as Captain Ivey's dredge boat *Suwanee.* According to the annual reports of the chief of engineers of the U.S. Army, these operations had not only widened the Eastern Pass of the Suwannee River near Cedar Key to accommodate larger steamboats but in 1890 had also led to the removal of snags, logs and some 527 cubic yards of rocks by *Suwanee* between Branford and Ellaville. This allowed more and larger boats to steam up to at least Hudson (now Dowling Park) in relative safety. Additional dredging work continued in the following years.

In or around 1893, the steamboat *Sam Pyles* arrived on the Suwannee River, complementing *Belle of Suwannee* and others. It had been built in 1885 at Panasoffkee, Florida, and was first owned by Sam Pyles, who traveled the Withlacoochee River (the one in central Florida) and its adjoining lakes. The Plant Investment Company, owned by Henry Plant, purchased the steamboat in December 1892. *Sam Pyles* had two decks and a stern wheel like many of the other steamboats on the Suwannee. It was small, only seventy-six feet by seventeen feet by about four feet (with a displacement of thirty-one tons in 1911); because of this, it carried few passengers, if any.

*Sam Pyles* was badly damaged and blown ashore during the 1896 hurricane. Refloated and repaired, it continued to operate on the Suwannee River and other nearby locations. In 1901, *Sam Pyles*'s hull and boilers were rebuilt for continued service according to an annual steamboat inspection report. In or around 1903, it was sold to a naval stores business based in Savannah before eventually being owned by the Gulf Coast Transportation Company, which operated the vessel on the Suwannee River at least part of the time. *Sam Pyles* remained in service until at least 1911, when it last shows up in an annual steamboat inspection report. The same report shows it as being home ported in Apalachicola but having been last inspected in late July 1910 at Branford. Among the captains during its time on the Suwannee River were E.T. Pooser, Robert Stapleton, Dan McQueen and Alf Davis.

Captain E.L. Magruder, hoping to compete with Captain Ivey, moved the steamboat *Louisa* to the Suwannee River in 1894. It had been built at Dublin, Georgia, in 1890, displaced 200 tons and was 101 feet by 25 feet by

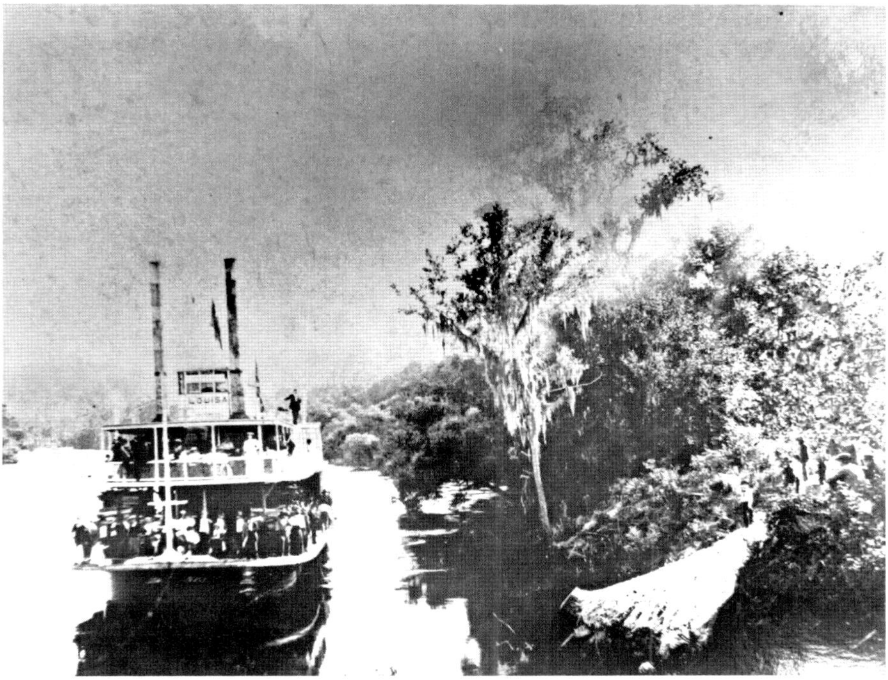

*Louisa* at Branford, circa 1895. *Suwannee County Historical Museum.*

5 feet in dimensions. Captain Magruder, in addition to owning *Louisa*, was also an owner and master on the profitable Chattahoochee-Apalachicola River route for many years. *Louisa* had several staterooms that gave *Belle of Suwannee* a run for its money. At some point after the devastating hurricane of 1896, Magruder sold *Louisa* to a company based out of Georgetown, South Carolina. *Louisa* continued in service in the Georgetown area until it apparently hit a snag and sank on the Santee River in October 1904, according to a 1905 annual report of steamboat activities.

The competition between Magruder and Ivey was heightened when Captain Ivey built his largest steamboat, *C.D. Owens*, in October 1895. It displaced 231 tons and was 135 feet long, 33 feet wide and had a draught of nearly 5 feet. The steamboat was named for Ivey's friend and an official of the Savannah, Florida & Western Railway, one of the predecessors of the railroad still running east and west through Live Oak today. The vessel's owner was the Suwannee River Steamboat Company, a partnership among Ivey and other businessmen. Unfortunately, Ivey's competition was short-lived due to the 1896 hurricane, and *C.D. Owens* was soon sold to the Independent Navigation Company (of which Magruder was a prominent partner). *C.D. Owens* was eventually transferred to the Chattahoochee-Apalachicola River run. However, the steamboat was destroyed by fire at Columbus, Georgia, in March 1899, taking two other steamboats with it.

## The Waning Years

The heyday of steamboating ended in late September 1896 after the "Great Hurricane of 1896" smashed through Florida on its way up the East Coast. Despite the turn of fortunes after 1896, several businessmen poured money and steamboats into the Suwannee River for a dozen more years. In these waning years of steamboating on the river, companies with names like the Independent Navigation Company, Suwannee River Steamboat Company and Suwannee River Operators Steamboat Company competed against (and, in some cases, merged with) one another for the reduced amount of business available to them. Captain Robert Ivey's impact on local steamboating lessened during this period as that of Captain E.L. Magruder increased. Sometime around 1898 (shortly after selling *Belle of Suwannee* to Magruder), Ivey bought the *C.U. Sheppherd* (also spelled "*Shepherd*"). The vessel had been constructed in Jacksonville in 1892 and had hauled phosphate on the Withlacoochee River (the central Florida one) before being sold to Ivey. The steamboat was small, built in the style of shallow-water tugs. *C.U. Sheppherd* displaced only twelve tons and measured fifty-two feet long, eighteen feet wide and had a draught of a little over three feet.

Captain Ivey owned *C.U. Sheppherd* for only about three years before selling it to the Suwannee River Steamboat Company in or around 1901. The 1903 *Blue Book of American Shipping*, a marine and naval directory of the day, states that the Suwannee River Steamboat Company made runs from Cedar Key to Hudson (now Dowling Park) twice a week with E.L. Magruder as manager. However, it did not own *C.U. Sheppherd* for long, as it was sold to the Gulf Transportation Company in 1902. By 1904, the small steamboat was no longer active.

Captain Magruder continued to operate steamboats on the Suwannee River alongside Robert Ivey before buying out most of Ivey's assets. In the fall of 1898, Magruder's Independent Navigation Company brought the steamboat *Thetis* onto the Suwannee River. *Thetis* was from Apalachicola, displaced 61 tons and measured 97 feet long, 19.5 feet wide and had a draught of 3.8 feet. It had one deck, but as far as historians know it never carried passengers. Dan McQueen, the famous mulatto pilot, worked for Magruder on *Thetis* for over a year and continued working for the Suwannee River Steamboat Company when it bought the steamboat in March 1900. An annual steamboat inspection report states that on July 11, 1903, while steaming on the Suwannee River, *Thetis*'s African American chief engineer, Peter Walker, fell overboard and drowned due to heart trouble. Accidents were common in an era when few people knew how to swim. *Thetis* plied the Suwannee River under a variety of companies until the winter of 1913, when it was finally dismantled.

A few months after *Thetis* began operations on the Suwannee River, the Gulf Transportation Company of Tampa introduced *City of Hawkinsville* as competition. *City of Hawkinsville* was the largest steamboat known to have ever operated on the Suwannee River. It was built in Abbeville, Georgia, in 1896 for the Hawkinsville Deepwater Boat Lines and displaced 319 tons, with measurements of 141 feet long, 31 feet wide and a draught of nearly 6 feet. *City of Hawkinsville* had two decks and originally two funnels but for most of its career sported only a single funnel. After completion, the vessel's maiden trip (which began on April 19, 1897, according to an old photograph) was to carry cotton from Hawkinsville, Georgia, on the Ocmulgee River. It then steamed between Hawkinsville and Darien, Georgia, on the Altamaha River, but in 1900, it was sold to the Gulf Transportation Company and moved to Florida. The steamboat was mainly used to tow barges of timber for the pencil factories located in and around Cedar Key on a route that usually included Branford, Clay's Landing, Old Town and, finally, Cedar Key.

Unfortunately for *City of Hawkinsville*, its entry into Suwannee River waters occurred at a time when Florida was experiencing a boom in railroad construction. Businessmen such as Henry Plant and Henry Flagler expanded railroad routes throughout Florida for the ever-increasing number of visitors, cutting into steamboat profits. The introduction of automobiles in the first years of the twentieth century further eroded steamboating's attractiveness, as people could now transport goods or go on excursions at much cheaper rates. Steamboats on the Suwannee River became fewer and fewer; many were either abandoned, sunk by disaster or transferred to more profitable waters.

The last known commercial steamboat to arrive on the Suwannee River was *Three States*, owned at the time by the Suwannee River Steamboat Company. It displaced 126 tons and measured 140 by 25 by 4.2 feet in size, with two decks and a stern wheel. *Three States* was built in 1898 in Apalachicola by the Independent Navigation Company (E.L. Magruder's company) and was named for the three states through which it originally traveled: Florida, Georgia and Alabama. Its service on the Suwannee River was brief, from May to October 1901, but it had an interesting career that bears noting.

Even before its time on the Suwannee River, *Three States* had been wrecked or suffered severe damage at least three times. In 1899, it struck a sandbar while some fifty-two miles downriver from Columbus, Georgia. The force of the current pushed *Three States* around and smashed part of the sternwheel. Captain E.L. Magruder believed the damage was too much to allow it to continue, so he boarded a train and returned to Columbus. In the meantime, the crew was able to repair the sternwheel enough for *Three States* to get to Chattahoochee, where repairs could be completed to allow it to finish the trip to Apalachicola.

The following year, in January 1900, *Three States* suffered a broken shaft on its port side. The crew managed to steam the vessel to Columbus after temporary repairs by disconnecting the port engine, placing a log under the shaft and running the starboard engine. It was fully repaired after this incident but was all but destroyed on December 5, 1900. *Three States* was docked at the Columbus wharf when firefighters found the steamboat with its upper works engulfed. A hole was cut into the boat's hull to sink it and douse the flames before they totally destroyed it. *Three States* had been valued at $15,000, but the fire caused $11,000 in damages. According to local newspaper reports of the day, "It is the opinion of the boat men that she is so badly damaged that she will never be worth anything any more. The machinery has been burned twice and is pretty badly out of shape, while the hull timbers are so badly burned as to make her valueless."

However, *Three States* was raised and repaired, then sent to the Suwannee River for its brief run in 1901 before returning to the Chattahoochee and Apalachicola River waterways. The Suwannee River Steamboat Company sold *Three States* to the Bainbridge Navigation Company, which in turn had sold it by 1905 to the Columbus (Georgia) Steamboat Association. While in that company's service, *Three States* filled in for five other steamboats when they were out of service for repairs between Columbus, Georgia, and Apalachicola, Florida. *Three States* was used so infrequently that more than once it was thought that it was abandoned, only for astonished onlookers to watch it gather up steam and sail by. It did not help that, according to the Georgia Archives, *Three States* again burned and sank at Columbus in 1906. It was then raised and repaired. The vessel operated for a year before yet again burning and being rebuilt. If the Georgia Archives is right about these two later burnings, *Three States* led a charmed (or cursed?) life, indeed. Despite infrequent use and multiple incidents, in 1907, it was stated to have carried the largest cargo of the season on the Chattahoochee and Apalachicola Rivers—269 bales of cotton, 2,500 shingles, 50 bundles of hides and 420 sacks of cottonseed, along with its regular crew and 20 passengers. The same year saw it make fourteen round trips between Columbus and Apalachicola carrying a total of 1,175 passengers.

By 1915, *Three States* had been sold to the Merchants' and Planters' Steamboat Company, which continued to use it on the Chattahoochee-Apalachicola River system. In 1918, the U.S. Army Corps of Engineers listed it as abandoned by its owners. However, the lucky steamboat made several more trips after that date. The *Apalachicola Times* newspaper noted the boat's arrival in the area in March 1920 after a long absence: "It looked like old times on the river to watch Captain Tom Whiteside reversing the gears and shooting the steam to the river steamer *Three States*." In 1922, steamboat inspectors arrived to inspect *Three States*, only to find the steamboat sunk at Columbus, Georgia. Its days of steaming were finally over.

## Steamboat Finale

Back on the Suwannee River, only *Thetis* and *City of Hawkinsville* survived after 1905. *Thetis* lasted until the winter of 1913, when it was finally abandoned. This left only *City of Hawkinsville* on the Suwannee River, but its days were numbered. After over twenty years of service on and around the Suwannee River, *City of Hawkinsville*'s last captain, M. Currie, abandoned it on May 19, 1922, according to its official registry records (some sources say it stopped steaming in 1914). One of its last jobs, according to legend, had been to transport railroad parts for the railroad bridge at Old Town near Fanning Springs. The completion of this railroad hastened the steamboat's demise. After being abandoned by Captain Currie, *City of Hawkinsville* gradually settled on the river's bottom some one hundred yards south of the railroad trestle at Old Town.

*City of Hawkinsville*'s upper works, which remained above water, were later removed as an obstruction to river travel, leaving its hull, machinery and sternwheel lying on the riverbed. In that condition *City of Hawkinsville* remains today, now one of Florida's few underwater archaeological preserves

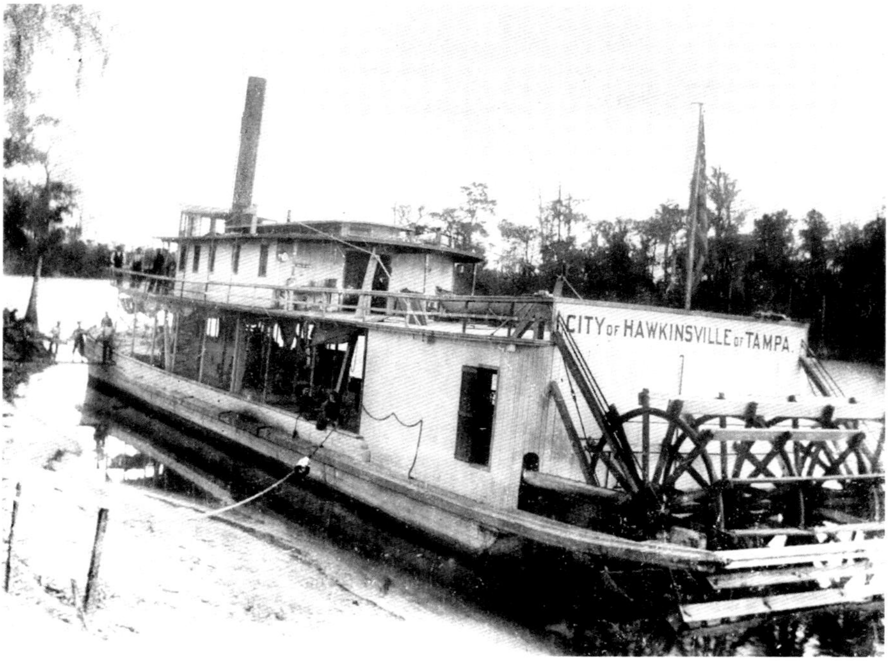


*City of Hawkinsville* on the Suwannee River, circa 1914. *State Archives of Florida.*

and a member of the national historic registry. Experienced divers can dive on the steamboat resting only a foot below the surface to see just a part of what life may have been like over one hundred years ago.

Commercial steamboating on the Suwannee River had lasted nearly one hundred years, but it simply could not compete with railroads, automobiles and shifting economies. Today, of the estimated fifty commercial steamboats that plied the Suwannee River, the wrecks of *Orpheus*, *Madison*, *David L. Yulee*, *City of Hawkinsville* and at least six other steamboats are still located just beneath the dark waters. *City of Hawkinsville*, as earlier noted, lies at Old Town. The remains of *Orpheus*, the first known commercial steamboat to steam upriver, lie where it sank in 1847; it is not too far from *City of Hawkinsville*. *David L. Yulee* remains where its owners abandoned it in 1885 in one of the river offshoots near the mouth of the Suwannee River. *Madison* (or at least a steamboat that most historians agree is *Madison*) is in Troy Spring, where it was scuttled in 1863. Visiting these wrecks can still evoke memories of long ago, when the grand boats slowly wound their way down upon the Suwannee River.

14

# THE IRON HORSE MAKES ITS MARK

Railroads have long been an important part of Suwannee County's history. Whether it was Live Oak, Wellborn, Branford, Dowling Park, McAlpin or O'Brien, practically every existing community (and many of those that no longer exist) owes its establishment to the railroads. Although most of the railroads that pushed through Suwannee County are long gone, their history remains. These railroads opened the vast forests and virgin lands of Suwannee County to industry and citizens alike.

## Pensacola & Georgia Railroad

The first railroad to come through Suwannee County was the Pensacola & Georgia (P&G) Railroad, which was chartered in January 1853 and completed in 1861. It ran from Tallahassee east, almost to Lake City, and also west to Quincy. The president of the railroad was Edward Houston (sometimes spelled Houstoun), for whom the community of Houston was probably named in 1859. Houston Street in Live Oak, one of the community's first streets, would be named for him, as well. Seeing that the first railroad depot in Live Oak was on the southeast corner of Houston and Conner Streets, it made the street name all the more appropriate.

The P&G operated throughout the Civil War, but the railroads in Florida were not connected to the rest of the Confederacy. This made it difficult to move troops, food and material to where they were most needed. To alleviate the problem, a connector line was built between Live Oak and Lawton (now DuPont), Georgia. It is part of what made Live Oak grow after the Civil War, as people traveling by rail had to travel through Live Oak to get to any other point in Florida. The unfinished connector line and the P&G railroad bridge across the Suwannee River at Columbus (now Suwannee River State Park) were the two major targets of the Federal troops who landed in Jacksonville in 1864. These troops were defeated in February at the Battle of Olustee, Florida's largest Civil War battle. Saved from the destruction, the P&G Railroad continued to shift men and materials through the northern part of the state. Unfortunately for the Confederacy, the connector line was not completed until March 1865, one month before the Civil War ended.

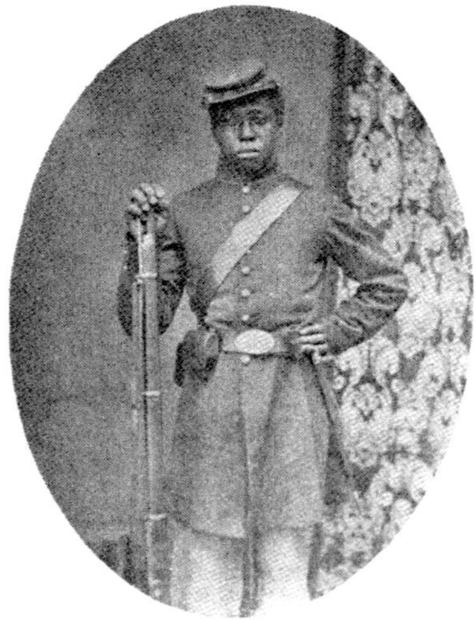

Private Robert J. Jones of the Fifty-Fourth Massachusetts Infantry Regiment. A farmer from Ohio, he was one of the Union soldiers missing and presumed dead at Olustee. *State Archives of Florida.*

In 1866, the Pensacola & Georgia sold its interests in the connector line to the Atlantic & Gulf Railroad, which linked to the P&G between Live Oak and Lake City. In 1868, financial problems caused P&G itself to be sold to notorious scalawag George Sampson, and in 1869, the railroad merged with the Florida, Atlantic & Gulf Railroad (formerly Atlantic & Gulf) to become the Jacksonville, Pensacola & Mobile Railroad. Sampson was assisted by carpetbagger Milton Littlefield, a former Union general who was known as the "Prince of Carpetbaggers" for his multiple accounts of fraud, embezzlement, lies and cheating.

In 1882, Sir Edward Reed purchased the Jacksonville, Pensacola & Mobile Railroad and renamed it the Florida Central & Western Railroad (FC&W). Two years later, Reed consolidated the railroad with others in Florida within the Florida Railway & Navigation Company, which in 1888 was renamed the Florida Central & Peninsular Railroad. The Seaboard Air Line Railway purchased a majority of the railroad's stocks in 1899 and leased the rest in 1900, before outright purchasing FC&W in 1903.

This ownership would last until the 1960s, when a merger with longtime rival Atlantic Coast Line was completed; the new entity became Seaboard Coast Line Railroad. In 1982, the railroad became part of the Seaboard System, which in 1986 was renamed the current CSX Transportation.

## LIVE OAK & ROWLANDS BLUFF RAILROAD

While Henry Plant was expanding his railroad empire in the 1870s and 1880s, other men were investing in Suwannee County. In 1881, the Live Oak & Rowlands Bluff Railroad was chartered. Its purpose was to continue the short Florida branch from Live Oak to Lawton farther into Suwannee County, reaching the Suwannee River at the community of Rowland's Bluff. That community would soon be renamed New Branford, after Henry Plant's birthplace of Branford, Connecticut. The "New" would later be dropped and it would carry on as Branford, Florida. The Live Oak & Rowland's Bluff Railroad, built with convict labor, would be consolidated with other Plant holdings in 1884.

## SUWANNEE RIVER RAILWAY COMPANY

Another railroad established during this time was the Suwannee River Railway Company. Louis Bucki, a timber partner of Governor George F. Drew, built the railway from Ellaville to Hudson-on-the-Suwannee (also known as "Hudson-upon-the-Suwannee" or simply "Hudson"), where it would connect with a steamboat to travel down the Suwannee River. The branch was completed by 1888, gradually making its way to Luraville, but it was not incorporated at the time.

The Suwannee River Railway was purchased by Edward J. Carter of New York City, along with Bucki's timberland in Suwannee County, and incorporated on February 15, 1895. Carter planned to improve the railway by putting in new rails, stock and equipment, as well as extending the line north to Jasper and south to Bronson and beyond. This would allow his railroad to access more of the phosphate mines that were being discovered at the time. As such, the capital for the project was listed as $1 million.

The Suwannee River Railway took out a full-page listing in an 1895 issue of the *Official Guide of the Railways* to show its projected routes. The railroad hauled timber to the big sawmill at Ellaville and limerock from quarries around Luraville and Fredericksburg (a community in Suwannee County that no longer exists). The line was being rebuilt and planned to reopen that year. At its height, the line operated only from Ellaville, on the Suwannee River, to Fredericksburg and from Flagler (another since-abandoned community) to Hudson-on-the-Suwannee, which later became Dowling Park. As with most railroads, actual mileage was far less than what was projected. Carter's plans never came to fruition, and the struggling line faded out of existence in the next few years. However, it continued to show up on maps for another ten years or so.

## LIVE OAK, TAMPA & CHARLOTTE HARBOR RAILROAD

The 1880s was a busy time for railroads in Suwannee County. In 1881, the Live Oak, Tampa & Charlotte Harbor Railroad was incorporated by Henry Plant and others to extend through New Branford and down to Tampa. However, Plant learned that there was another railroad already chartered for a similar route (the Florida Southern Railway) when the two groups literally ran into each other while building their tracks (Plant's line was going south, while Florida Southern's was headed north). Plant negotiated a deal with Florida Southern's investors in December 1883 so that there would be no competition. Florida Southern would give up its charter to build north of Gainesville, Plant would not build south of Gainesville and Plant would financially help the Florida Southern to build its route to Charlotte Harbor. Within six months, Plant had absorbed both of these railroads, as well as others (including the Live Oak & Rowland's Bluff Railroad), into the Savannah, Florida & Western Railway.

The Savannah, Florida & Western Railway was part of the Plant System, the unofficial name given to the vast holdings of Henry Plant that included not just railroads but also steamboats and hotels. When Plant died in 1899 at the age of eighty, he was buried in his birthplace of Branford, Connecticut. His railroad empire was sold to the Atlantic Coast Line Railroad for $46.5 million. With over 2,200 miles of track, it was the largest railroad system in operation in the nineteenth century.

## Lake City & Suwannee Railroad Company

Not all incorporated railroads were as fortunate; some railroads never survived long enough to see a mile of track laid. On December 22, 1859, for instance, the Florida legislature authorized the incorporation of the Lake City & Suwannee Railroad Company, with the commissioners for the new company being John Eccles, John R. Herndon, Z.M. Paschall, Noble A. Hull, Edward R. Ives, William B. Ross, Calvin Peacock, James W. McQueen and Arthur J.T. Wright. Hull and Peacock were Suwannee County residents, as were possibly one or more of the others. The company was authorized to construct a railroad from Lake City to New Boston, or some other point on the Suwannee River below its head of navigation, with a capital stock of $200,000. New Boston was upriver from present-day Branford at the bend of the river west of Little River Springs. It was also situated across from Lafayette County's seat of McIntosh (otherwise known as New Troy). The legislature allowed the Lake City & Suwannee Railroad Company three years to begin construction of the railroad, with completion within five years. Most likely because of the coming war, nothing was apparently done on the railroad. It would not be the last time an incorporated railroad in the Suwannee County area failed to materialize.

## Suwannee & Gulf Railroad Company

A similar fate befell another railroad nearly thirty years later. On June 2, 1887, the legislature also incorporated the Suwannee & Gulf Railroad Company, whose line started at the Savannah, Florida & Western Railway in New Branford and ran through Suwannee, Alachua and Levy Counties to its terminus at Cedar Key. The original charter members of the Suwannee & Gulf were Robert Y.H. Thomas, James E. Richards, Fred A. Wolfe, James S. Bodiford and James O. Andrews, all of Florida, as well as Henry C. Benson of New York. In 1891, the Florida legislature approved the continuation of the railroad's rights and privileges for another three years. However, as with many railroads of the time that were incorporated, this company's work fell through shortly thereafter. Henry Plant was not allowed the rights to the railroad depot terminus in Cedar Key, so he merely established another railroad to Tampa instead. This resulted in the decline of Cedar Key as a major port in Florida.

## LIVE OAK, LURAVILLE & DEADMAN'S BAY RAILROAD

At the same time that the Savannah, Florida & Western Railway was increasing its mileage in the 1880s and 1890s, Suwannee County locals Thomas and Robert L. Dowling were expanding their business investments in the area. One of the main catalysts for an increase in railroads in the 1890s was the discovery of phosphate near Luraville. In 1893, Thomas Dowling was one of several men who established the Live Oak, Luraville & Deadman's Bay Railroad to access the rich phosphate mines that sprang up almost overnight. Dowling was president, Thomas I. McIntosh (who also ran a large phosphate mining company in Luraville) was vice president, Frank White was secretary and Lewis Dowling was treasurer. James D. Taylor was also involved in the incorporation of the railroad. The railroad's plan was to pass from Live Oak through Luraville, then continue on into Lafayette and Taylor Counties until ending at or near Deadman's Bay, a distance of sixty miles.

Half of the railroad was constructed for use as Dowling's log road, but financing for the other half never materialized; only the grade of the railroad was completed from the end of Dowling's logging railroad to Luraville nine miles away. This hampered the shipment of phosphate from Luraville to the various railroad lines leaving Live Oak. The incomplete roadbed and assets of the Live Oak, Luraville & Deadman's Bay Railroad were purchased by the Live Oak & Gulf Railway Company in 1895, but not the charter itself.

## LIVE OAK & GULF RAILWAY COMPANY

The Live Oak & Gulf Railway Company was chartered in 1895 by men from New York and Citra, Florida (near Ocala). R.L. Anderson of Ocala was president; Charles W. White of Citra, Florida, was vice president; and James R. White of Citra was secretary and treasurer. These three men also made up the board of directors. The Live Oak & Gulf quickly took over the assets of the incomplete Live Oak, Luraville & Deadman's Bay Railroad, going so far as to hire Thomas McIntosh and others who had been part of the older railroad. The new railway made money mainly from the phosphate mines at and near Luraville, but by 1897, it was determined that the phosphate had too much iron content and was worthless for its intended purpose as a fertilizer. The railway languished for several years as other schemes came to

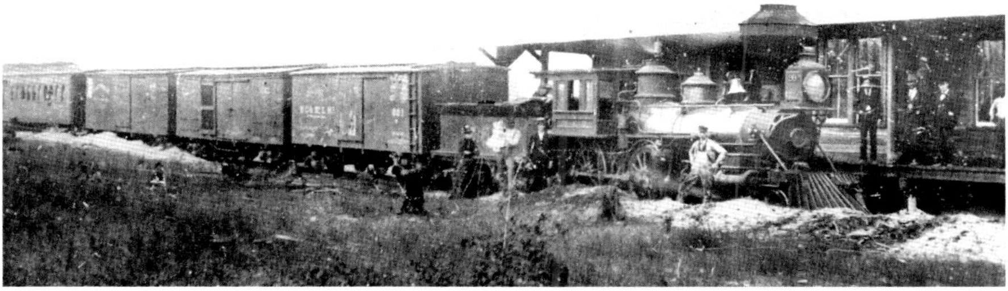

Live Oak & Gulf Railway train at Luraville, circa 1896. A Jim Crow–era segregated passenger car brings up the rear. *Suwannee County Historical Museum.*

naught due to competing railroads. Some money was made between 1899 and 1902, however, by carrying phosphate and railroad materials for other railroads. The railway was purchased by the Southern Investment Company and, in 1905, merged with the Suwannee & San Pedro Railroad.

## THE DREW FAMILY AND THE SUWANNEE & SAN PEDRO RAILROAD

Another prominent family in the development of Suwannee County railroads was the Drew family. George Franklin Drew was born in Alton, New Hampshire, in 1827. He moved to Georgia and opened a machine shop in Columbus in 1847. Drew was against secession, despite living in the South and marrying a Southerner. After the war, he looked at moving to Brazil but stopped once he arrived at the Suwannee River. Determining that there was money to be made in the area, Drew built what at the time was the largest sawmill in Florida and established the community of Ellaville on the Madison County side of the river. Drew was elected governor of Florida in 1876 as Reconstruction ended.

The Suwannee & San Pedro (S&SP) Railroad was incorporated in 1899 by H.W. Sweet of Baltimore, Maryland, and R. Bowen Daniel, Augustus V.S. Smith and E.C. Bixler, all of Jacksonville. The railroad would be built across the Suwannee River from the Live Oak & Gulf Railway, whose current terminal was near Luraville. The Drew family, needing railroads for its multiple sawmills in the Suwannee Valley area and beyond (other than their small logging spurs that they already had in abundance), purchased the

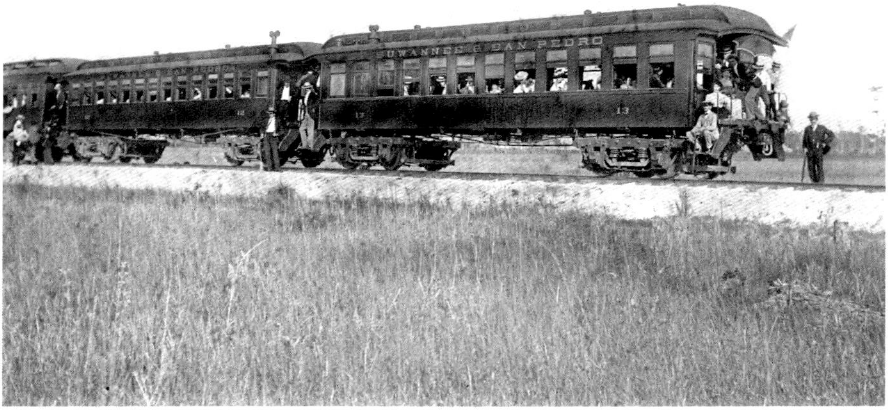

Suwannee & San Pedro Railroad cars between 1899 and 1902. *State Archives of Florida.*

Suwannee & San Pedro Railroad charter a little over three months later for about $2,500. The Drews realized that the Live Oak & Gulf Railway wished to span the Suwannee River into Lafayette County; purchasing the S&SP was a way for the Drew family to stop the competition. Shortly before the death of Governor Drew in 1900, the charter was amended to extend the route from Live Oak to Mayo, Perry and Deadman's Bay. After Governor Drew's death, his sons Frank and George pushed headlong into work on the railroad, purchasing thousands of acres in Taylor and Lafayette Counties for logging after another railroad defaulted on its work. The railroad used a three-foot narrow-gauge rail instead of the more usual five-foot rail. It merged with the Live Oak & Gulf Railway and the Alton Branch Railway (named after George F. Drew's birthplace of Alton, New Hampshire) to form the Florida Railway in 1905.

## ST. MARYS, SUWANNEE & GULF RAILWAY

In 1903, George and Frank Drew, along with T.P. Alston and R.N. Ellis, organized the St. Marys, Suwannee & Gulf Railway, which was intended to start in Nassau County and go through Charlton County, Georgia, then pass through the Florida counties of Baker, Columbia, Hamilton and Suwannee to Live Oak. The line would then run southwesterly through Suwannee, Lafayette, Taylor, Jefferson and Wakulla Counties. The railroad came about because of a conflict between the Drew family and the Seaboard Air Line Railway (SAL). Unfortunately for the family, the SAL got wind of the negotiations and purchased part of the route before the Drew family and its railroad holdings could come up with the money to do so. The St. Marys, Suwannee & Gulf Railway was thus yet another railroad to die a premature death due to funding issues and conflicts.

## FLORIDA RAILWAY

The Florida Railway came about as a merger between the Suwannee & San Pedro Railroad, the Live Oak & Gulf Railway and the Alton Branch Railway in 1905. It was yet another railroad venture by the Drew family. The railway struggled with its competitors (especially the Live Oak, Perry & Gulf Railroad) and because of Frank Drew's stubbornness, which caused issues with both the Atlantic Coast Line and the Seaboard Air Line. Drew's attempts to expand the railway to places such as Jacksonville failed, as the investment companies that had the money for the railway were unwilling to loan the money to Drew, because it would compete with their other railroads, such as the SAL. It did not help Drew's fortunes when his local rival, Thomas Dowling, purchased many of the sawmills from which the Florida Railway had been receiving money.

The Florida Railway finally ceased operations in 1916, well behind on payments. Unpaid employees were even sabotaging the railroad tracks at this point! About all that remains of the Florida Railway is its bridge across

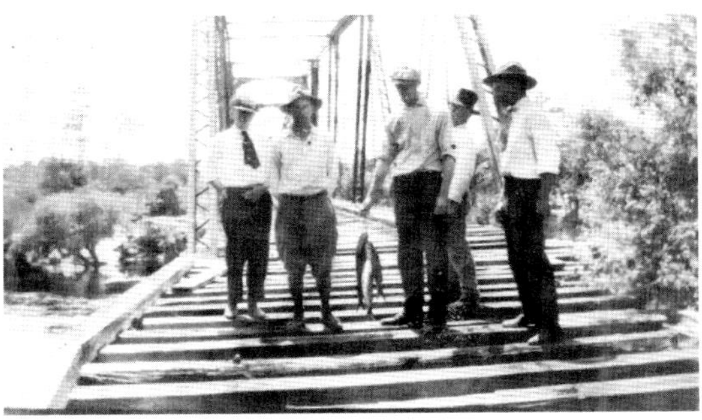

Fishermen on the abandoned Florida Railway bridge over the Suwannee River near Wilmarth, circa 1920s. The locals used it as a fishing dock. *Susie Baxter.*

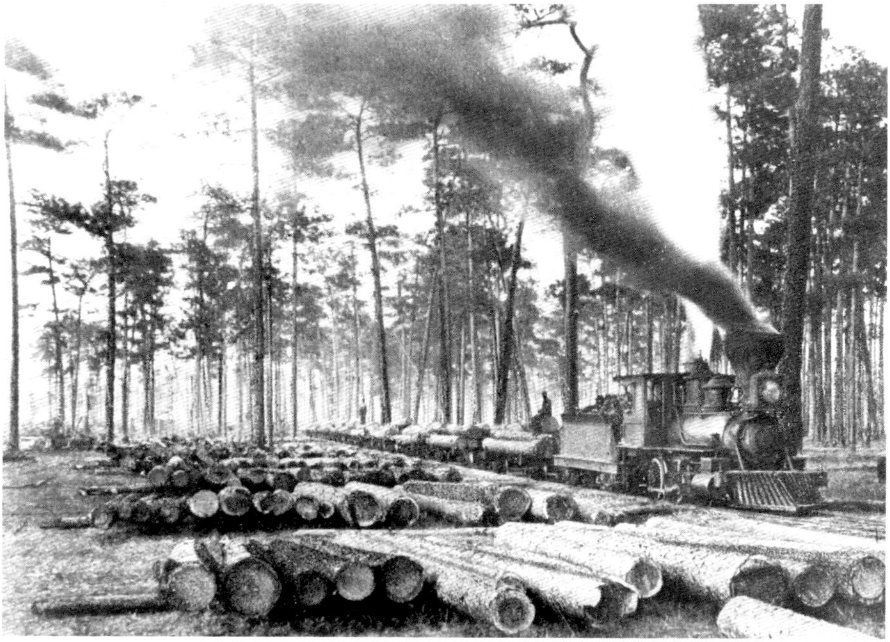

Logging virgin pine timber in Suwannee County, circa 1900. *State Archives of Florida.*

the Suwannee River between Luraville and Branford, at a place that was once called Wilmarth. Today, it sits deserted, a reminder of one of the many railroads that failed in the South.

The SAL could have bought the railroad at this time and linked it with one of its other railroads to make a large sum of money, but the railroad's hatred of Frank Drew was so great that it did nothing but sit back and watch the Drew empire crumble. It takes great resentment for a for-profit company to see an easy opportunity to increase its revenues but decide to do nothing, just to see a man's wealth disappear.

## R.L. DOWLING SHORT LINE

The R.L. Dowling & Sons Lumber Company began in Live Oak in the 1890s with Thomas Dowling and his nephew Robert L. Dowling, who soon built a logging railroad from Live Oak westward. The sawmill was in the northwest part of town and connected with both the Plant System (later ACL) and the

Florida Central & Peninsular (later SAL) Railroads. As the logging railroad marched westward to cut out the timber, it was renamed the R.L. Dowling Short Line. By about 1900, the railroad had reached the Suwannee River at Hudson-upon-the-Suwannee. The community was named Dowling Park in honor of the family that brought so much commerce to it. As the timber was cut in the region, the railroad expanded into Lafayette County.

## LIVE OAK & PERRY RAILROAD

In 1903, the Dowling Short Line was approached by Skelton Williams, president of the Seaboard Air Line, who wished to use the short line in his battles with the Drew family and its nearby Suwannee & San Pedro Railroad. Williams urged Dowling to incorporate. As a result, Dowling's logging railroad incorporated as the Live Oak & Perry Railroad on September 23, 1903, but it could not complete its line to Perry because of a lack of funding brought about by Williams's removal from SAL.

## LIVE OAK, PERRY & GULF RAILROAD

The Atlantic Coast Line also wanted to enter the profitable region between Perry and Live Oak, but it had been held up by an old agreement between the Plant System and the Florida Central & Peninsular. To get around it, the ACL financed the new railroad for preferred traffic in an agreement between the ACL and all the Dowlings' lumber and railroad interests in 1905. A new charter was created that replaced the faulty Live Oak & Perry charter, and on June 16, 1906, the famous Live Oak, Perry & Gulf (LOP&G) Railroad was incorporated.

The early years were good for the LOP&G, as it had good resources through the ACL and good revenue as the railroad extended past Perry to a place called Flint Rock, seventy-four miles from Live Oak. It took until 1921 to get there, however. According to one railroad expert, the Live Oak, Perry & Gulf carried more lumber-related traffic during its history than probably any other railroad in Florida.

In 1918, the LOP&G was sold to the ACL, which sold it in 1928 to Brooks-Scanlon Corporation, owners of a large sawmill in Foley (in Taylor County).

**BETWEEN LIVE OAK AND HAMPTON SPRINGS**

**TIME TABLE No. 3**

In Effect Sunday, Aug. 18, 1907, at 12:01 A. M., Superseding Time Table No. 2, Dated May 19, 1907.

| WEST BOUND—Read Down: Second Class, Freight and Passenger | Second Class, Freight and Passenger | First Class, Passenger | Passenger | Passenger | Passenger | Passenger | Car Capacity Sidings | Miles | STATIONS | Miles | EAST BOUND—Read Up: First Class, Passenger | Passenger | Passenger | Passenger | Passenger | Second Class, Freight and Passenger | Freight and Passenger |
|---|---|---|---|---|---|---|---|---|---|---|---|---|---|---|---|---|---|
| 3 A. M. | 7 A. M. | 11 A. M. | 9 A. M. | 5 P. M. | 1 P. M. | 13 P. M. | | | | | 2 A. M. | 12 A. M. | 14 P. M. | 6 P. M. | 16 P. M. | 4 P. M. | 8 P. M. |
| Daily ex. Sun. | Daily ex. Sun. | Sunday Only | Sunday Only | Sunday Only | Daily ex. Sun. | Sunday Only | | | | | Daily ex. Sun. | Sunday Only | Sunday Only | Sunday Only | Sunday Only | Daily ex. Sun. | Daily ex. Sun. |
| Leave | Leave | Leave | Leave | Leave | Leave | Leave | | | | | Arrive | Arrive | Arrive | Arrive | Arrive | Arrive | Arrive |
| 7.45 | 11.10 | 8.40 | 11.10 | 2.00 | 5.00 | | | 0 | LIVE OAK | 49 | 10.28 | 11.50 | | 6.15 | 9.00 | 4.25 | 6.00 |
| | | | | | | | | | S. A. L. CROSSING t | | | | | | | | |
| 8.05 | 11.30 | 8.58 | 11.20 | 2.10 | 5.18 | | 5 | 6.5 | f STARR | 42.5 | 10.06 | 11.30 | | 5.37 | 8.42 | 4.00 | 5.33 |
| 8.10 | 11.35 | 9.02 | 11.05 | 2.22 | 5.20 | | 7 | 8.5 | f MERCER | 40.5 | 10.01 | 11.25 | | 5.53 | 8.37 | 3.58 | 5.29 |
| 8.15 | 11.40 | 9.06 | 11.38 | 2.25 | 5.25 | | 13 | 10 | f PLATT t | 39 | 9.53 | 11.22 | | 5.50 | 8.34 | 3.50 | 5.25 |
| 8.30 | 11.50 | 9.15 | 11.48 | 2.36 | 5.36 | | 28 | 14 | f LANCASTER | 35 | 9.47 | 11.12 | | 5.42 | 8.28 | 3.35 | 5.10 |
| 9.00 | 12.15 | 9.25 | 11.58 | 2.40 4.00 | 5.40 | 5.36 | 16 | 17 | s DOWLING PARK t | 32 | 9.40 | 11.05 | 2.15 | 5.35 | 8.18 | 3.15 | 5.00 3.40 |
| 9.05 | 12.30 | 9.29 | 12.03 | 4.04 | 5.49 | 5.39 | 24 | 18 | CHANCEY | 31 | 9.30 | 10.57 | 2.10 | 5.25 | 8.06 | 3.05 | 3.15 |
| 9.10 | 12.35 | 9.36 | 12.10 | 4.11 | 5.56 | 5.45 | 3 | 20.7 | f MAYO JUNCTION t | 28.3 | 9.23 | 10.50 | 2.01 | 5.18 | 8.00 | 3.00 | 3.05 |
| 9.20 | | 9.40 | | 4.15 | 6.00 | | 15 | 22 | s DAY t | 27 | 9.20 | 10.47 | | 5.15 | | 2.56 | |
| 9.35 | | 9.47 | | 4.20 | 6.05 | | 6 | 25 | f SILO | 24 | 9.13 | 10.40 | | 5.08 | | 2.49 | |
| 9.40 | | 9.54 | | 4.25 | 6.10 | | 7 | 28 | f TOWNSEND t | 21 | 9.05 | 10.32 | | 5.01 | | 2.40 | |
| 10.00 | | 10.11 | | 4.43 | 6.28 | | 13 | 33 | f SMITH t | 16 | 8.47 | 10.14 | | 4.43 | | 2.23 | |
| 10.20 | | 10.30 | | 5.01 | 6.46 | | 5 | 38 | f FENHOLLOWAY | 11 | 8.29 | 9.56 | | 4.25 | | 2.07 | |
| | | | | | | | | | FLORIDA RAILWAY CROSSING | | | | | | | | |
| 10.25 | | 10.38 | | 5.07 | 6.52 | | 7 | 40 | s BLUE CREEK JUNCTION t | 9 | 8.23 | 9.50 | | 4.20 | | 2.00 | |
| 10.40 | | 10.49 | | 5.17 | 7.02 | | 16 | 44 | s PERRY d | 5 | 8.16 | 9.40 | | 4.10 | | 1.50 | |
| 10.55 | | 11.00 | | 5.30 | 7.15 | | 8 | 49 | HAMPTON SPRINGS | 0 | 8.05 | 9.30 | | 4.00 | | 1.30 | |

**MAYO BRANCH**

BETWEEN MAYO JUNCTION AND ALTON

| 3 | 7 | 11 | 9 | 5 | 1 | 13 | Car Capacity Sidings | Miles | STATIONS | Miles | 2 | 12 | 14 | 6 | 16 | 4 | 8 |
|---|---|---|---|---|---|---|---|---|---|---|---|---|---|---|---|---|---|
| | P. M. Leave | | P. M. Leave | | | P. M. Leave | | | | | | | P. M. Arrive | | P. M. Arrive | | P. M. Arrive |
| | 12.35 | | 12.10 | | | 5.45 | | 20.7 | f MAYO JUNCTION t | 14.3 | | | 2.01 | | 8.00 | | 2.55 |
| | 12.47 | | 12.20 | | | 5.55 | 16 | 25.5 | f DELL | 9.5 | | | 1.51 | | 7.50 | | 2.40 |
| | 12.55 | | 12.25 | | | 6.02 | 5 | 28.5 | f PETERSON | 6.5 | | | 1.44 | | 7.44 | | 2.32 |
| | 1.05 | | 12.35 | | | 6.07 | 18 | 32.7 | s MAYO d | 2.3 | | | 1.35 | | 7.35 | | 2.20 |
| | 1.15 | | 12.40 | | | 6.17 | | 35 | ALTON d | 0 | | | 1.20 | | 7.30 | | 2.15 |
| A. M. | P. M. | A. M. | P. M. | P. M. | P. M. | P. M. | | | | | A. M. | A. M. | P. M. | P. M. | P. M. | P. M. | P. M. |
| Daily ex. Sun. | Daily ex. Sun. | Sunday Only | Sunday Only | Sunday Only | Daily ex. Sun. | Sunday Only | | | | | Daily ex. Sun. | Sunday Only | Sunday Only | Sunday Only | Sunday Only | Daily ex. Sun. | Daily ex. Sun. |
| 3 | 7 | 11 | 9 | 5 | 1 | 13 | | | | | 2 | 12 | 14 | 6 | 16 | 4 | 8 |

s Regular Stop. f Flag Stop. d Telegraph Station. t Telephone Station. Trains Nos. 2 and 4 handle United States Mail and Southern Express.

East-bound Trains have right of track over West-bound Trains of same class. (See Standard Rules.) Mayo Branch Trains will get clearance at Dowling Park and Mayo Junction, and all trains going on Mayo Branch will register and report to Dispatcher at Mayo Junction. All trains must approach the trestle or bridge at Suwannee River at a speed slow enough to come to a stop within one hundred feet distance at any point. All trains MUST COME TO A FULL STOP at Florida Railway crossings at Fenholloway and Mayo, S. G. & W. C. Ry. at Perry, and at S. A. L. Ry. crossing, Live Oak. Yard Limit at DOWLING PARK will extend from a point six hundred feet from east end of "Y" to the west end of trestle. Yard Limit at LIVE OAK will extend from S. A. L. Railway Crossing to Passenger Station, and no train will exceed a speed of ten miles an hour while in yard limits.

All Trains will register at Blue Creek Junction.

Sidings not on Time Card—43 Mile Post, 6 cars; 44 1-4 Mile Post, 3 cars; 34 1-2 Mile Post, 5 cars; 48 Mile Post, 3 cars; 57 Mile Post, 2 cars; T. C. N. R. Spur, 2 cars.

J. LEE ENSIGN, President. S. T. GRIMSHAW, Superintendent. G. B. GLOVER, Chief Dispatcher.

Timetable for the Live Oak, Perry & Gulf Railroad, August 18, 1907. *Suwannee County Clerk of Court.*

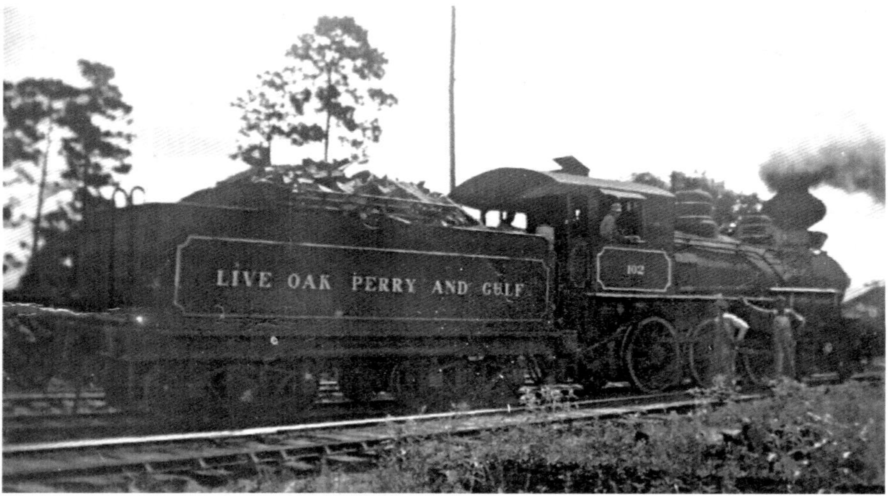


Engine No. 102 of the Live Oak, Perry & Gulf Railroad, circa 1940. *Suwannee County Historical Museum.*

Over the years, the railroad served a variety of purposes. For instance, corn, cotton, watermelons and tobacco were transported from Suwannee County. June was always a particularly busy month for the LOP&G, because that is when watermelons were shipped from Suwannee County. Gradually, passengers left as automobiles became cheaper and more available. In 1954, Brooks-Scanlon sold the LOP&G to the Southern Railway, which merged it with the Georgia Southern & Florida in 1971 to create the Live Oak, Perry & South Georgia Railway. The railroad was sold to the Gulf & Ohio in 1994 (which called it the Georgia & Florida) and was later sold to the Georgia & Florida Railnet.

## THE LURAVILLE LOCOMOTIVE

As the major railroads updated their rolling stock in the late 1800s and early 1900s, they would sell their old locomotives to some of the numerous logging companies that availed themselves of the rich timber in Suwannee County and the surrounding areas. One of those logging companies was Bache & Hagen (also called Bache Brothers), whose operations centered on Luraville and spanned both sides of the Suwannee River.

One of these old locomotives was a ten-ton, wood-burning 4-4-0 model built between 1850 and 1855 (probably by Danforth-Cooke). The 4-4-0 designation means that the locomotive had four leading (and smaller) wheels followed by four driving wheels and no trailing wheels. This steam engine was used to haul timber for the lumber company for several years until it ended up in the Suwannee River.

The exact cause of how the locomotive wound up in the Suwannee River is still up for debate: it could have jumped the railroad track or even been deliberately dumped there after logging operations ceased. The most likely cause was that the locomotive was being transported by barge between Suwannee and Lafayette Counties (since Bache Brothers owned timberlands on both sides), and it fell into the river. Because the engine was so old, it was not worth hauling up.

Whatever the true reason, the locomotive's remains sat on the riverbed, all but forgotten for many years. James Lancaster, a resident of Luraville, saw the engine during a drought as a child and always remembered it. In 1979, now much older and with funding, Lancaster raised the locomotive from the riverbed and parked it near his home in Luraville. The engine was eventually donated to the State of Florida. Partially restored, the steam engine continues to sit in front of the Florida Department of Agriculture and Consumer Services Laboratory Complex in Tallahassee. It is one of the oldest surviving locomotives in the United States.

By the end of the first decade of the twentieth century, railroad expansion in Suwannee County was coming to a close. Many of the earlier railroads were abandoned as automobiles took over more of the market and as larger railroad companies bought out smaller ones. Despite this, there would be one more new railroad established during this period in Suwannee County.

## SUWANNEE RIVER & WHITE SPRINGS RAILWAY

In 1909, the Suwannee River & White Springs Railway was chartered by locals W.L. Tedder (president), C.H. Tedder, H.E. Barcus (vice president), W.W. Pennington, C.D. Blackwell (secretary and treasurer) and H H. Brown. The purpose of the short line railway was to carry passengers and freight from Live Oak to White Springs, a distance of sixteen miles. However, a 1910 railroad report showed that the railroad had only four and a half miles of tracks with a value of $9,000 (about $226,000 in 2016 dollars), plus $5,000 (about $126,000 in 2016 terms) in rolling stock. The railway lasted only about three years; it does not show up on any annual state railroad reports after 1912.

After the introduction of the automobile and better roads, railroads became less necessary to transport goods. Gradually, the lines that had survived the late 1800s and early 1900s were abandoned, merged with others or were sold out to other entities. Today, CSX Transportation is the only railroad running through Suwannee County, ironically along the same route as its ancestor, the Pensacola & Georgia Railroad, the very first railroad that ran through Suwannee County before the Civil War.

# 15

# CONVICT LEASING SYSTEM

The end of the Civil War found Florida in dire financial straits. The effects of Reconstruction exasperated these effects, so much so that in 1876, the state's prison system was in shambles. Prisoners were being housed in old buildings that were long due for replacement, but money was not available. The federal government, in the Compromise of 1876 (also called the Compromise of 1877, because that is when it took effect), ended Reconstruction in some parts of the South (including Florida) in exchange for the selection of Rutherford B. Hayes as president. This occurred despite the fact that Samuel Tilden had received approximately 250,000 more popular votes than Hayes and was only one electoral vote shy of outright winning the election.

## Convict Leasing Begins

In 1877, George Franklin Drew became governor of Florida after a tumultuous election. He was the first post-Reconstruction governor for the state and lived across the Suwannee River at Ellaville; however, he owned land and businesses in Suwannee County. As a way to balance the budget and to help struggling private companies get back on their feet after the end of slavery, Drew signed a law allowing the state to lease prisoners to private companies on a massive scale. These companies would then be responsible

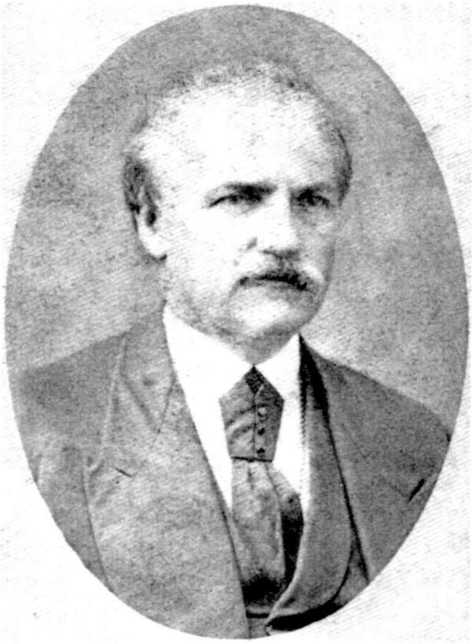

Governor George Franklin Drew, the first post-Reconstruction governor of Florida. He lived across the Suwannee River and owned acreage and businesses in Suwannee County. The photograph is circa 1875. *State Archives of Florida.*

for the housing, feeding and care of the prisoners. It was a win-win situation for the state: not only would it no longer have to care and house the prisoners (saving some $25,000 per year at the time), but it would lease them out to the highest bidder, bringing revenue into the state's depleted coffers. Many states enacted similar laws; Alabama had been the first to lease prisoners, all the way back in 1846, and would be the last to repeal the law in 1928.

Unfortunately, the system was ripe for abuses. A result of the convict lease system was that a large number of African Americans were convicted of crimes and sent into the labor camps, while many whites were able to pay their fines or otherwise escape the penalties. And unlike many (but not all) slave owners who had seen their slaves as major investments and treated them decently by the standards of the day, private companies had no incentive to treat the prisoners well. In some ways, the convict leasing system was a type of slavery that endured beyond the legal end of slavery.

A book entitled *American Siberia* was written in 1891 by J.C. Powell, who had been captain of one of the convict camps in Florida. Much of the book deals with the convict leasing system in Suwannee County, where for many years half of the state's entire prison population was sent to work in turpentine and timber plants and railroad building.

The book begins at the railroad depot in Live Oak:

> *In the fall of 1876 a singular spectacle might have been observed at the little town of Live Oak, in Northern Florida. A train had just arrived, and from one of the cars some thirty odd men disembarked and formed in irregular procession by the road-side. The sun never shone upon a more abject picture of misery and dilapidation. They were gaunt, haggard, famished, wasted with disease, smeared with grime, and clad in filthy tatters. Chains clattered about their trembling limbs, and so inhuman was*

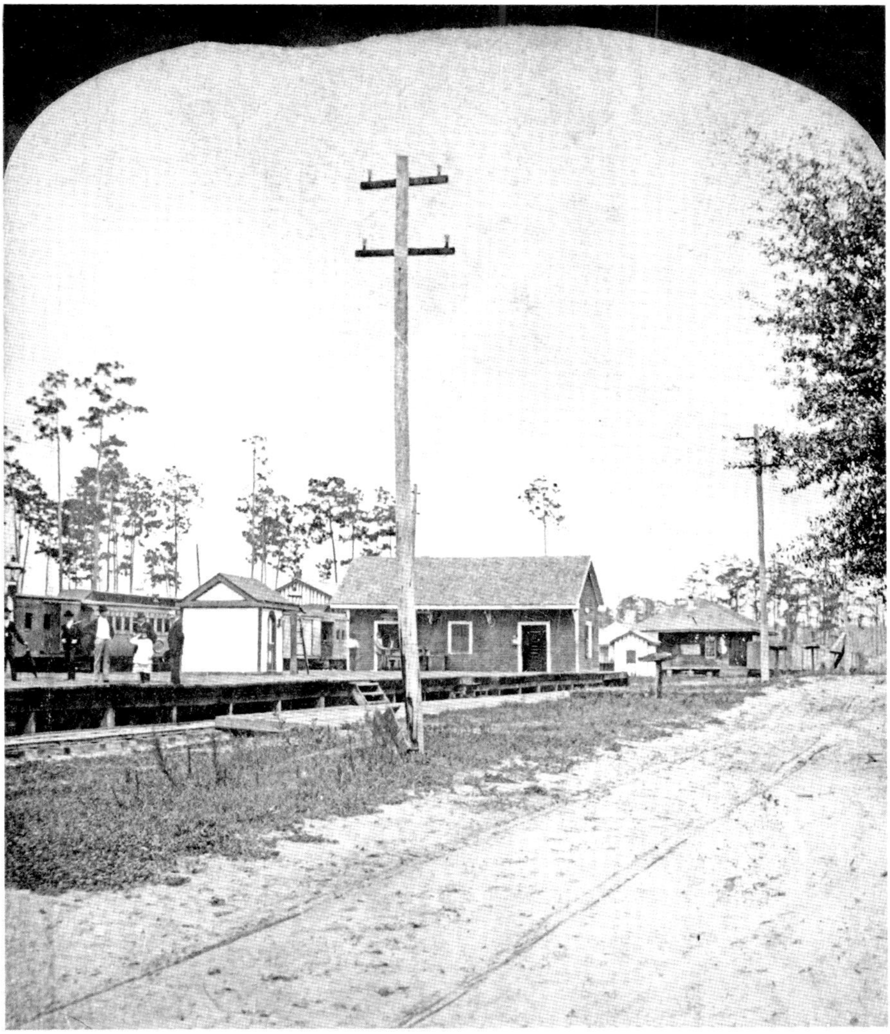

Live Oak Railroad Depot in August 1877. *State Archives of Florida.*

> *their aspect that the crowd of curiosity seekers who had assembled around the depot shrank back appalled.*

Captain Powell discusses in detail some of the abuses (torture) that the prisoners had suffered in other parts of the state, including "sweating," "watering" and "stringing." "Sweating" involved shutting up the prisoner in a small box of a cell without ventilation or light; the heat would be nearly unbearable. "Watering" was, as Powell called it, "the celebrated torture practice during the Spanish Inquisition under the name of 'ordeal by water.'" Prisoners were strapped down, a funnel placed in their mouths and water poured in. The prisoners' stomachs would distend from the pressure and would place pressure on the heart. "Stringing" was hoisting up a prisoner by their thumbs and letting them dangle until cut down. Powell mentions that some of the prisoners in his care had thumbs that were as long as their index fingers and swollen at the tips due to repeated abuses. Death was common from these torture treatments.

## Padlock and Sing Sing

The prisoners who arrived in Live Oak by train were taken by Captain Powell to a location near the Santa Fe River. There, they began working in timber under lease from Major Henry A. Wyse (also spelled Wise) of Live Oak. Several months later, Wyse subleased his prisoners to the Live Oak firm of Dutton, Ruff, and Jones, which dealt in turpentine, among other endeavors. Charles K. Dutton, formerly of New York City, was the man behind the firm. The prisoners were sent to the convict camp of Padlock, where they first built their sleeping quarters. Powell goes into some detail describing the sleeping arrangements for the prisoners, noting that there were platforms not unlike steamship berths to sleep on. The prisoners were chained together; after bedtime, they could move only with the permission of the guards.

Padlock was a crude camp. As with most convict camps of the time, there were no fences. Guards stationed around the perimeter with loaded weapons were usually enough to stop fleeing prisoners, although some would try and succeed. Cooking was done under a lean-to shelter, "hunter-fashion," as Powell called it. The food was the fat of bacon (Powell called it "white bacon"), corn bread and cowpeas. Powell mentioned that the food was not prepared well and speaks of scraping a large number of gnats off the food in the summer before he could eat it. Conditions, although better than they had been under state care, were still brutal.

Once the timber around Padlock had been worked over, Powell and his prisoners moved about four miles away and built a new camp, named Sing Sing, after the notorious New York prison. This camp was an improvement over Padlock, although still rough even by the standards of the day. The conditions of the convict camps were bad enough that some prisoners would intentionally maim themselves to escape the hard work; some would die from infections of their own doing. Others would risk their lives to flee the camp. Many would be recaptured, while others were killed by the guards. A few very unlucky prisoners would flee into the woods and swamps, never to be seen alive again. One prisoner's tattered clothing and bones were found by hunters about six months after he had disappeared. But the fate of most escapees remains unknown to this day.

Since convict life was so brutal, some prisoners resorted to violence in an attempt to escape. Powell mentioned one such event in his book. It involved W.J. (Winder Josephus) Hillman, a guard who became a captain of the convict camps; later, he would leave the convict business and become a millionaire.

The incident that Powell wrote about took place when Hillman was still a young guard at the convict camp. He had managed to upset nearly all the white convicts (Powell does not cite the reason). Three convicts, Columbus See, John G. Lippford and John Williams, concocted an outrageous scheme to escape the camp. First, Columbus See managed to become the cook of the camp by ingratiating himself to the guards. This allowed him more or less free rein of the camp, and he used it to his advantage. Rifle cartridges began disappearing one at a time, but the guards assumed it was a result of their using the cartridges during hunting, as many were prone to do.

One day, while Hillman was the only guard really on duty (there was one more, but he was the night watchman, asleep in his bunk; a third had gone hunting), there were only a few convicts still at the camp. See passed by Hillman as if he was going to run an errand but then grabbed him and fought for the guard's gun. Hillman would have retained control of the gun had it not been for See's two co-conspirators, who disarmed him. Hillman was knocked to the ground, and See threatened to shoot him.

The sleeping night watchman was disarmed, and the convicts dug up the rifle cartridges that See had been burying in the yard, one at a time, for weeks. Several other convicts joined the original trio. Before escaping, See first went to kill the assistant cook because of a grudge he had against him. The assistant cook realized what was happening and ran into the woods in the direction of the guard who had gone hunting. Frustrated in one murder attempt, See returned to Hillman, still lying on the ground surrounded by the other convicts, and determined to shoot him. One of the other co-conspirators, Lippford, was able to convince See not to kill Hillman, as it would lead to them all being executed if they were caught.

See, Lippford, Williams and five other inmates decided to make their escape from the camp and made haste while singing at the top of their lungs. Seven or eight inmates decided that an escape was foolhardy and remained behind. Captain Powell's house was nearby, and his wife watched all that happened from the front door. She grabbed a pistol and accosted one of the runaways as he made his way past the house. "Jim, go back to camp!" she told him. Powell wrote that the convict replied, "Can't do it, Miss Lizzie; dis yere too good a chance!"

Once the escapees had made their way out of sight, W.J. Hillman picked himself up off the ground, grabbed the pistol that Mrs. Powell offered him and borrowed a horse to begin the chase. At the same time, the guard who had been hunting was coming back to camp, having been alerted of the escape by the assistant cook. Powell reported in his book that Hillman was so black in the face from what he had just endured that the other guard mistook him for another escaping African American and nearly shot him before Hillman shouted out his name as he was passing by.

When Powell returned to the camp, a posse was gathered, but they lost track of the inmates at the Suwannee River. Powell noted in his book that he was not able to capture any of the escaped inmates, although he heard about their movements through other means. Lippford went to Marion County, where he cleared a little place in the woods and lived. In time, local law enforcement found out about Lippford's past and tracked him down. He fled and was shot by a local posse, although he staggered into the surrounding swampy wilderness and was never seen again. Powell believed that "it is safe to say that his bones lie somewhere in the dark morass that swallowed him up."

Williams also died a violent death, having moved to Brooksville and hidden for some time. Eventually, he became bold and would venture out in public. In a drunken stupor, he shot an African American dead for no reason and was then chased down by citizens and law enforcement. A running gunfight ensued, with a deputy sheriff finally shooting Williams dead.

The third conspirator, Columbus See, still had not been captured when Powell wrote his book. Powell believed that See was in Taylor County, terrorizing people in the woods like a madman. Attempts to retrieve him were unsuccessful. The life of a prisoner was tough, but the life of an escaped prisoner was even tougher.

Another incident Powell described in detail concerned an escape attempt by two prisoners. They had managed to outrun the guards and were doggedly followed by a one-armed trusty named Jesse Simpkins who, for whatever reason, was intent on stopping them. He was a powerful man despite the loss of his arm, and the guards depended on him in emergencies. As a result, Simpkins was not liked by the other convicts, who saw him as a spy. His numerous invented stories did not help him in such matters.

The two prisoners, originally fleeing the convict camp, now determined to rid themselves of Simpkins once and for all and made several unsuccessful attempts to trap and kill him. Simpkins was able to outrun or outwit the prisoners, who then resumed their attempt to escape. Eventually, the two prisoners reached the Suwannee River, with Simpkins close behind. Night and freedom were near.

The first prisoner jumped into the river, swam across and emerged on the other bank, calling for his associate to do the same. The second inmate jumped into the river, with Simpkins remaining on the riverbank behind him. With one arm, Simpkins would have had a difficult time crossing the river, and the prisoners would have made quick work of him. Instead, Simpkins did about the only thing he could do. He picked up a large stone and hurled it at the second prisoner's head that was now bobbing across the river to safety. Simpkin's aim was true, and "he cracked the man's skull like paper, and splattered his blood and brains into the water," as Powell put it. The corpse began tumbling over and over as the current pushed it downriver. The prisoner who had already made it across the Suwannee River turned tail and fled into the woods, not wanting to be caught by the powerful Simpkins.

Simpkins made the long trek back to the convict camp; Powell and the other guards assumed that Simpkins had joined the first two prisoners and made his escape. Simpkins told Powell the story of how he had chased the two prisoners for miles and then killed one with a stone. Due to Simpkins's predilection for telling tall tales, nobody believed him. However, about a week later, Governor George Drew, who lived near the current Suwannee River State Park, contacted Major Henry Wyse (the person who had been leasing the convicts) to report that the body of a convict had been pulled from the water with a skull fracture. The corpse was identified as the man whom Simpkins had killed, and the guards thereafter believed his stories.

Powell writes in his book that in the post-Reconstruction era, the administration of state law was rather loose. He specifically points out Alachua County, which appeared to "regard the prison as a sort of clearing-house for its pauper incumbrances [*sic*]." He noted that while at the Sing Sing convict camp in Suwannee County, he received from Alachua County

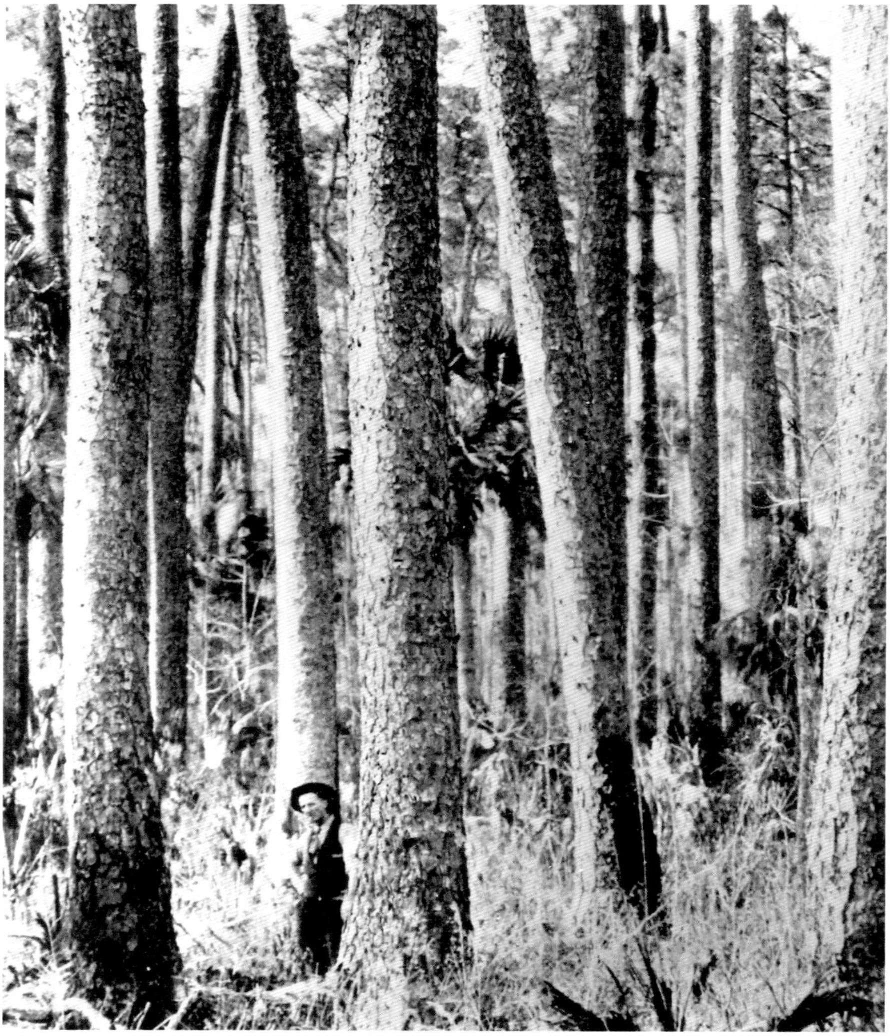

Some of the virgin timber from which convicts would drain turpentine, circa 1900. *State Archives of Florida.*

a blind prisoner. The prisoner had been accused of stealing a gun, which Powell wryly noted would not have done him much good. The man did well in the convict camp, spending the majority of his time working at the pumps. When his sentence was over, he stayed in Suwannee County and made a good living cutting timber; he had a knack for hitting the trees in the right spot even though he couldn't see them.

One of the interesting stories from *American Siberia* concerned a prisoner named John Key West. He was named after the location where he was convicted. Key West had a healthy appetite for gopher tortoise, which at the time was seen as a type of delicacy (and which probably contributed to its endangerment over the years). "Boiled, fried, stewed, or fricasseed, it was all one to him, and the unfortunate gopher that he encountered in the forest might as well give himself up for lost," Powell wrote.

One day, John Key West had finished his day's work on the chain gang and was allowed to go to a neighboring hill to look for gopher tortoises. Nothing awry was noticed until the guard collected his prisoners at the end of the day and realized that Key West was not among them. The guard sent a trusty to look for him. The trusty got to the hill where Key West had said he was going and found nothing but his hat and a trapped gopher tortoise. Upon closer examination, the trusty noticed that some nearby sand was disturbed, so he began digging. It was not long before he unearthed a human foot and ran back to tell the guard.

The guard and his prisoners arrived at the site and recognized the shoe on the foot as belonging to John Key West. They could not pull him out of the dirt, and a neighbor living nearby refused to give the guard a shovel because he thought it would be used to bury prisoners. The group had to dig with their tools and hands until they finally unearthed the body. Key West had apparently been so zealous in tracking a gopher tortoise that he had followed it into its hole and dug through until he was buried alive when the tunnel caved in. The most interesting part of the story was that once they pulled John Key West out of the hole, they found clutched in his lifeless hands the second gopher tortoise!

## RAILROAD CONSTRUCTION

After some time away, Captain Powell and his convicts returned to Suwannee County under the lease of railroad tycoon Henry Plant. His company, the Plant Investment Company, included what came to be called the Savannah, Florida & Western Railway, which ran through Suwannee County. The company wished to expand its railroad lines and began construction of the Live Oak & Rowland's Bluff Railroad.

As the convicts began construction of the railroad, not everyone was in favor of the new mode of travel. There was one "obstinate old man" named

Bill Harrison who had claimed "squatter's title" to some property and built a small store there, despite not having the legal right. He had the weapons to back up his claim, and the railroad company did not want to cause trouble. It offered to move Harrison's store out of the way, but he simply stated that he would kill the first person to lay hands on his building.

Captain Powell decided to continue building the railroad and laid the tracks up to one side of the store and then restarted them on the other side. A locomotive steaming along the line would have run right through the store. Eventually, Powell was given authority to move the store by any means necessary. Powell made one more attempt to negotiate with Harrison, but to no avail. Harrison and his assistant barricaded themselves inside the store and threatened to kill the first man who stepped inside.

Captain Powell had dealt with hotheads before and simply ordered his guards to surround the store and shoot into it if Harrison opened fire. With guards posted, Powell ordered his convicts to lay skids and then commenced to pull the store out of the way using ropes. The old store's timbers creaked and groaned, and then the structure began to move. After traveling ten feet, several loose boards fell on top of Harrison and his assistant, and they rushed out, indignant. "Dog gone you fellers! I believe you would tear a man's house down right over his head!" he yelled to Powell and his men. Powell and his convicts moved the store the necessary distance, nailed up the loose boards and continued their railroad construction.

Railroad construction was a dangerous business, one of the reasons that convicts (and, before the Civil War, slaves) were used to build them. The Live Oak & Rowland's Bluff Railroad was no different. Jesse Simpkins, the one-armed convict mentioned earlier, was one of the inmates tasked with building the railroad. One day, he was preparing to couple a locomotive, front first, to the rest of the train. He was also holding some oranges, and as Powell stated, "his attention was somewhat divided between his duty and the safety of the fruit." The locomotive's pilot (more familiarly called the cowcatcher) caught Simpkins and ran over him, lifting the engine's front wheels off the track. Powell found Simpkins wedged into a ball with the cowcatcher over him, part of the weight of the locomotive on top of him.

Assuming Simpkins dead, Powell had the remaining convicts move the locomotive so that they could get to the body. Within moments, they had raised the front of the engine enough to pull out Simpkins. To Powell's amazement, Simpkins stretched out, felt his body for injuries and then asked about his oranges! Other than a sore back for a few days, Simpkins was fine;

when Powell wrote his book in 1891, Simpkins was a free man and "sound as a dollar."

While constructing the railroad down to Branford, Powell recounted how there were still many people in the woods who knew little beyond their immediate affairs. He pointed out that "a man who would venture to tell them that the earth moved instead of the sun, or that there was a device by which a message could be flashed for leagues across a wire, would run the risk of being lynched, as too dangerous a liar to be at large." As a result, many people came out of curiosity to see the work on the railroad as it traveled farther south.

One backwoods family had heard rumors of railroads and came to visit Powell; he pointed out the railroad tracks and told them to wait for the engine to arrive. The family sat on the ground, nervous and excited, until they heard the engine's whistle. Their color left them and they scooted closer together as they waited anxiously. The engine was pushing a line of flatcars ahead of it, and the first thing the family saw was the flatcars. "Sakes alive! What's movin' them little houses with wheels onto 'em?" one of the women screamed. When the engine appeared, massive and belching smoke, the group hopped up and crowded around the man of the family in terror; they very nearly ran off into the woods. Powell remarked that one experience with the railroad was enough for them, and they never returned.

After the railroad was completed, another old settler in the area by the name of Hays was subpoenaed to be in Jacksonville for a trial. A U.S. marshal arrived to take him to Jacksonville, and he had no choice but to go. When Hays was told that he would have to ride by train, he was concerned, never having been on one before. He was dragged up the steps into the railroad car for the trip to Jacksonville.

When the train began moving, Hays burst into tears. He explained in between his sobbing "that he was no coward; he had faced destruction a thousand times in the woods and killed more bears than could be packed into that passenger coach, but the idea that he would never see his wife and family again filled him with sorrow." After being consoled by the marshal, Hays appeared to be doing better until the train coupled with another car with the usual jolt. Hays leaped from his seat. "Thar, she's struck a stump! Just as I knowed she would! Lord a-mighty! I'll never see Betsey agin!"

## An Odd Inmate

Captain J.C. Powell saw many things during his years in charge of the convict camps, but one incident was unparalleled. He received a female prisoner from Lake Butler. When the woman arrived, she was revealed to be a rather voluptuous African American woman with gaudy clothing who went by the name of Marietta Williams; Powell placed her in the women's quarters.

The next day, Marietta went to the commissary to retrieve a thimble. Powell watched her walk back to her quarters and noticed that her shoulders seemed to be too wide, her hips too narrow and her feet too large. Powell thought about it for a while until he determined to find out if Marietta was indeed a woman. He sent for his assistant, W.J. Hillman, to investigate with him.

Powell and Hillman entered the women's quarters and ordered all the other women to leave the room; he then told Marietta his suspicions. Marietta protested but at last was discovered to be a young man with a smooth face and slight build. He then explained himself; he was a part of an organized gang of thieves who operated in the larger towns of north Florida. To allay suspicions, they would dress as women during the day to determine their next target and then move in at night.

Unfortunately for "Marietta," he had gotten into some sort of scrap with a man while dressed in women's attire and had been unable to change before his arrest. Not knowing what to do, the prisoner carried on the deception throughout his arrest and trial before Powell found him out. The cross-dressing prisoner was given men's clothing and moved to the male housing, where there were already several members of his gang being held. He died of an unknown sickness while at the convict camp; doctors could do nothing to help him.

Powell learned later that "Marietta" had been hired by a well-known doctor in Live Oak as a servant girl, presumably so he could case the place before stealing from them. "Marietta" served the family well and then moved on; the doctor and his family frequently spoke of "her" as an exceptionally good girl. When they finally learned the truth about their servant "girl," the doctor and his family were horrified!

## A Life Turned Around

Other inmates were eventually able to change their lawbreaking ways. One such person was William Tyner, who had been sentenced to a short stint at the convict camp. While working in the woods, he and another inmate attempted to escape; Tyner was able to get away, and the other was shot and captured. This would have been the end of the story, but six months later, a wild-looking backwoodsman arrived at the convict camp to speak with Captain Powell. Powell received him to learn that the man was the brother-in-law of William Tyner. The brother-in-law said that Tyner was tired of running and wanted to come back and serve the rest of his sentence. Powell, surprised, told the man to have Tyner come back and serve.

However, it would not be that easy. The brother-in-law stated that Tyner hated to be whipped (one of the usual punishments for attempted escapes) and asked that Powell agree not to whip him. Powell agreed, and the man went off. He returned the next day, looking "foolish," as Powell put it. Powell asked where Tyner was, and the brother-in-law again stated emphatically that Tyner was deathly afraid of being whipped. Captain Powell reiterated that he had agreed not to whip him when he returned. After some back-and-forth discussions, the brother-in-law asked for a written agreement. Powell went to his office and drew up a formal promise not to whip Tyner when he returned, and this seemed to satisfy the brother-in-law.

The next day, Powell saw William Tyner coming down the road toward the convict camp. He had a belt full of ammo and a large pistol on his side. "Good morning, Captain," Tyner said a little sheepishly. After the usual pleasantries, Tyner unbuckled his pistol belt and handed it to Powell. "I guess I have no further use of this," he said. Powell took the weapon and ammo, then sent Tyner to change into prison garb. When Tyner returned to have his chains placed on him, Powell decided against it and instead made him a trusty with free rein of the camp. Tyner served out the remainder of his sentence without trouble and then was hired to work at the camp as a guard!

Not all inmates were treated so well within the state. The convict leasing system itself was fraught with various abuses. In 1921, a young man, Martin Tabert, died in Dixie County due to a financial mishandling and the cruelty of his overseer. The countrywide public uproar brought to light the abuses of the practice, and Governor Hardee (of Live Oak) signed a bill into law finally outlawing the practice, which ended in 1923.

## 16

# FORMER TOWNS AND LOST COMMUNITIES

Over the years, Suwannee County has been blessed with a number of communities. Some of these developed into full-fledged towns and cities, while others wilted away into nothing. In between these two extremes are several communities that continue to be an important part of Suwannee County's history, even if they are not as large as they once were.

## LITTLE RIVER/WELLBORN

The community of Wellborn is one of the oldest existing communities in Suwannee County; the area in and around it was settled by American citizens before practically any other location in the county. Historians would say that the present community of Wellborn began around 1830, when George E. McClellan claimed 560 acres at Wellborn's present site along the Old Spanish Trail. At the time, Native American attacks were still common in this frontier area of Florida. While the first homes were under construction, a lookout was posted to warn of Seminole Indian raids. McClellan's plantation home soon became a stop for stagecoaches traveling between St. Augustine and Pensacola; it was where horses were changed out and injured travelers (from the Seminole Indian attacks) were treated. McClellan called his community "Little River," after a short river that ran from McClellan Lake into what is now Wellborn Lake. Little River shows up on several maps until the 1870s, when the name "Wellborn" first appeared with and then replaced it. Interestingly enough, by the 1880s, there would be another community named Little River located due south of Wellborn and east of McAlpin, only about five miles from the original.

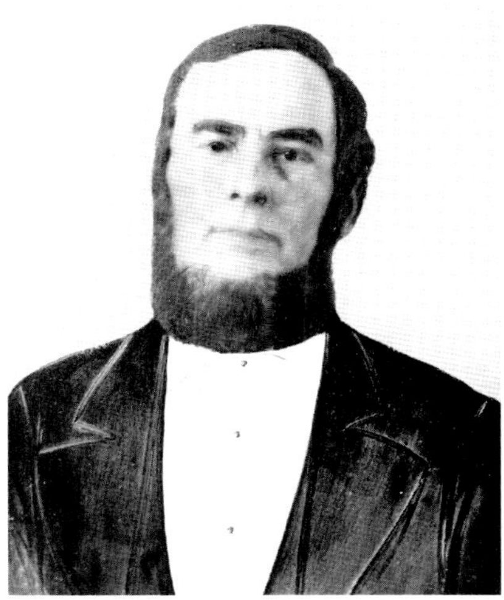

George E. McClellan, circa 1838. *State Archives of Florida.*

The Second Seminole War broke out at the end of 1835, and several battles and massacres occurred in north and central Florida. By September 1837, problems with Seminoles in northern Florida required detachments of soldiers to be stationed at Charles' Ferry (now Charles Springs), a nearby plantation, and on the Madison County side of the river at San Pedro. This threat had disappeared almost completely by the summer of 1838, as most Native Americans were moved elsewhere. Most of the soldiers and militia units were either disbanded or moved to areas of greater military activity, and the settlers who had fled to fortified outposts returned to their homes. But the danger was not over for the residents of north Florida. The last recorded Indian raid in Suwannee County was near present-day Wellborn in February 1842. In that month, the wife and several children of Richard "Dick" Tillis (called "Tullis" or "Tulli" in some accounts) were massacred while he was helping a neighbor. A full account of the attack, as well as George McClellan's letter to the governor petitioning for military assistance, can be found in the minutes of the 1842 session of the Legislative Council of the Territory of Florida.

Several "forts" were listed as being in modern-day Suwannee County during the Second Seminole War, although most were probably no more than a few logs set up as breastworks and barricades. Columbia County pioneer George Gillett Keen, in his published reminiscences, mentions a Fort Jinks at modern-day Wellborn. After the end of the Second Seminole War in 1842, this presumed fort, as well as the others in the area, were abandoned and soon stripped of all useful equipment by nearby settlers whose numbers increased with the threat of Indian attacks now gone. Today, little remains of these forts and outposts except a few scattered relics and place names (Fort White, Fort Lauderdale, etc.).

Due to the increasing number of settlers in the area, the Florida legislature petitioned the federal government in mid-December 1856 to establish a mail route "from the House of Geo. E. McLellan's [*sic*] on Little River in Columbia County to Shoal Town on Suwannee River, via Samuel Barber's and Wm. Johnson's, a distance of thirty miles." Since a map from 1856 already showed "Little River P.O.," either Little River already had a post office (the most likely explanation) or the mapmakers were Johnny-on-the-spot with the map. Little River continued to have a post office through the Civil War, but its days as a community were numbered.

In 1857, construction began on an east–west railroad across north Florida, with the portion running through Suwannee County being known as the Pensacola & Georgia Railroad. The railroad was completed in 1861, linking Jacksonville with Tallahassee and beyond. One of the civil engineers who worked on building the railroad was Louis Wellborn DuBois (also spelled "Lewis Dubose" or Dubois"), of Tallahassee. According to an old story often repeated, in appreciation for his help, DuBois was given 162 acres near the town that would bear his name. However, Suwannee County deed records actually show that DuBois purchased 240 acres on January 16, 1860, from the public lands of the State of Florida; the price was $1.25 per acre. DuBois quickly surveyed and platted the town of Wellborn in 1860 (spelled "Welburn" or "Wellbourn" on some period maps), as also recorded in Suwannee County's deed records.

It appears from a cursory review of Suwannee County records that DuBois did not retain ownership of the 240 acres that originally composed Wellborn, as he sold his acreage to more than a dozen different families within a year. One of those families who purchased property was the McLeran family, one of the most prominent families in Wellborn's history. According to some sources, the first post office at Wellborn was established in 1860 with Jesse N. McLeran as postmaster; however, other sources list October 17, 1865, as the establishment date. In 1884, A.W. McLeran opened a general mercantile store before serving as a state senator from 1893 to 1897; the store remained a family business until it was sold in 1967. The McLeran House, built around 1900, still stands as a popular bed-and-breakfast.

The completion of the Pensacola & Georgia Railroad through Suwannee County in 1860–61 (besides indirectly giving the community its name) allowed Wellborn to expand as settlers availed themselves of the railroad access that ran through the middle of the village. On November 27, 1863, in the midst of the Civil War, the Florida legislature corrected the original boundary line between the counties of Columbia and Suwannee. The correction affected

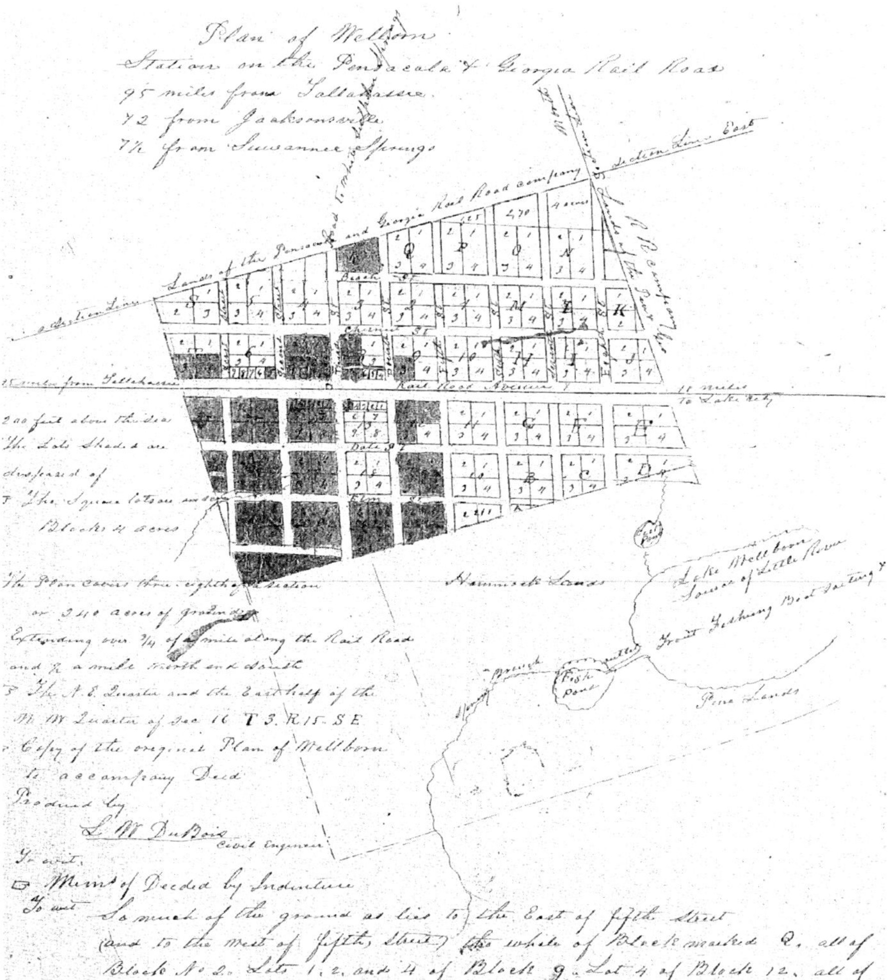


Recorded plat map of Wellborn, 1860. *Suwannee County Clerk of Court.*

the entire town of Wellborn (spelled "Welburn" in the legislative act); all of its residents would be considered citizens of Suwannee County. The community's location on the eastern border of Suwannee County, coupled with the old county line, had proven problematic for citizens who didn't know if they lived in Columbia or Suwannee County!

By the end of the Civil War, Wellborn was steadily growing, in part because of its easy railroad access. Meanwhile, the older community of Little River, only a mile or two south of Wellborn, struggled to continue its thirty-plus-year existence. The death knell of Little River sounded in 1866, when George E. McClellan passed away. McClellan was Little River's founder, prominent business owner and postmaster. With McClellan's death, Little River's fate was sealed. The older community remained on maps until at least 1874, however.

Wellborn played a role in the selection of the permanent county seat, since at the time it was one of six polling places in the county. The first election was held on March 27, 1869; none of the sites gained a majority of the votes, and there were problems with the voting. Individual polling site results are not shown in the minutes, but no doubt the majority of Wellborn citizens would have voted in favor of Houston, due to its proximity. A second vote held in May showed a majority of Wellborn's citizens voting in favor of the old courthouse lot in Houston.

It appears that during the period of the late 1860s and early 1870s, Wellborn had a good number of citizens (including many children) living within easy traveling distance. The Suwannee County Board of Public Instruction (commonly called Suwannee County School Board) was organized on July 9, 1869, as a result of an act of the 1869 legislature. It was not until September, however, that a quorum could be held. In that first meeting, Wellborn was one of only two schools authorized at the time. From that point on, Suwannee County children were able to attend one of the increasing number of schools located in various communities around the county.

A statistical paper published in New York City in 1884 showed Suwannee County as having eighteen post offices, with the major communities being Live Oak, Branford and Wellborn. According to some sources, between the mid-1800s and early 1900s, Wellborn boasted some 250 families within a ten-mile radius and was surrounded by a variety of orchards. One of the largest orange groves in Suwannee County was that of Wellborn-area citizen W.A. Tison, who also served in a number of government positions. Orange groves were widespread in north Florida until hard freezes in 1886, 1894–95 and

1899 wiped out the area's crops and forced orange farmers to relocate farther south. Northerners frequented a popular hotel located in Wellborn during this time, finding the climate and nearby Wellborn Lake a wonderful setting to spend winters. The town was also a major shipping point for poultry, eggs, cotton, grain and vegetables. By the end of the 1800s, a railroad spur ran from Wellborn to White Springs, where it received products from local lumber manufacturing plants, among other businesses.

During this heyday of Wellborn, a number of businesses operated in the "downtown" area. These included gristmills, cotton gins, general merchandise stores, boardinghouses, saloons, physicians and drugstores, blacksmiths, coopers, shoemakers, livery stables, sawmills and a millinery. Numerous farms also dotted the landscape around Wellborn, selling their wares in local markets. In the early twentieth century, the population density of the major communities had not changed, as period papers still showed Live Oak, Branford and Wellborn as the county's major population centers. Wellborn was supposedly the first community in Suwannee County with brick paving. A road three-quarters of a mile long and one block north of old Highway 90 (now CR 10A) was built sometime in the early 1900s (one source states 1916, another says 1917); a portion of the road still exists today in Wellborn.

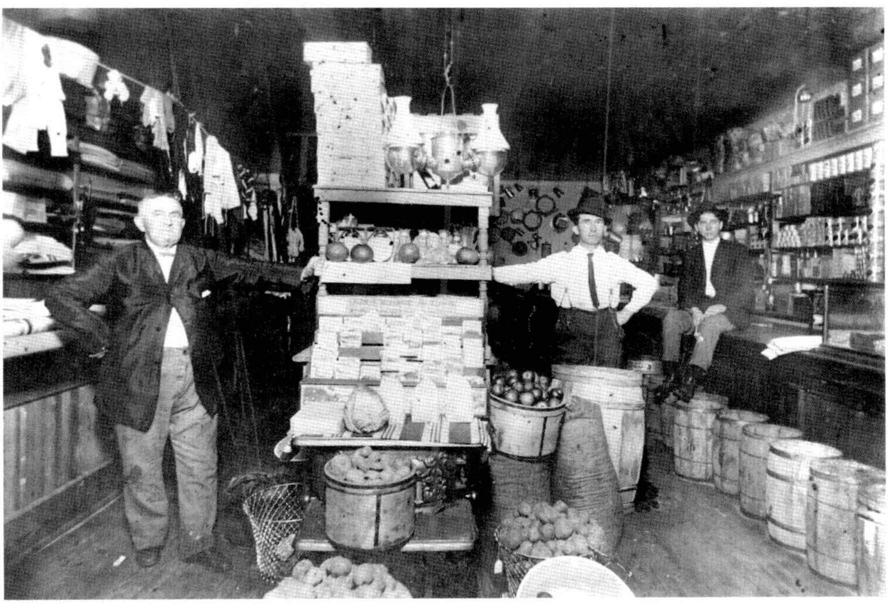

Cash Mercantile Company in Wellborn, circa 1880. *From left to right*: S.D. Hemming, Paul Hemming and Elmer Mosley. *Advent Christian Village Archives.*

Because of its continuing growth, the town of Wellborn was incorporated in 1903 with its own mayor, town council, marshal, clerk, tax collector, tax assessor and treasurer. In 1907, the charter was amended to take into account changes in the laws of Florida. In 1910, the Wellborn Bank opened, with E.B. McLeran Sr. as president and $15,000 in capital.

Unfortunately, Wellborn's growth was short-lived. By the late 1920s, the reduction in the number of cotton gins, lumber mills and turpentine stills; the destruction of the area's cotton crop by the boll weevil; and a population shift to south Florida meant that most people moved elsewhere. As a result, the town of Wellborn unincorporated in 1928 and has remained so ever since. The Wellborn Bank was also a victim of shifting population centers, closing at the end of 1928. Live Oak native and former governor Cary A. Hardee, president of the Commercial Bank of Live Oak, purchased the Wellborn Bank with the stipulation that the cashier, Merle Jernigan, continue in that position. The money and records of the Wellborn Bank were moved on Christmas Day 1928 in order to be open for business the next day.

At one time in its history, Suwannee County had more than one hundred schools in operation, mostly one-room buildings with one teacher and about a dozen pupils each. Over the years, the Suwannee County School Board consolidated these small schools into larger population centers as automobiles and better roads made travel more convenient. By 1960, only seven schools remained, Wellborn among them. However, the Wellborn school closed at the end of the 1966–67 school year; its remaining students were bused to Live Oak or Branford.

Today, Wellborn is a quiet residential community, but its annual Blueberry Festival attracts thousands of people from surrounding areas. Despite the loss of some older structures due to fire and demolition over the years, several historic buildings continue to grace the Wellborn area, including the McLeran House, the McLeran Store, the George Walters House, the Bailey House and the "Old Brick Store."

## Luraville

Luraville was settled in 1878 and had a population of seventy-five in 1886. Colonel Washington Lafayette Irvine, who operated a ferry there, named the community for his then five-year-old daughter, Lura (also spelled "Laura") Irvine. Unfortunately, Lura Irvine was horribly burned in a girls' dormitory

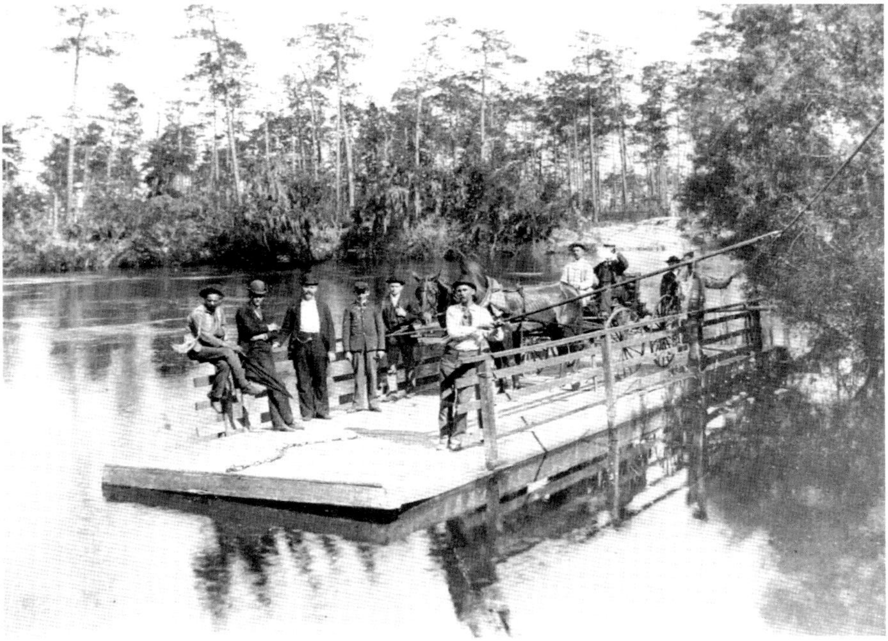

Irvine's Ferry at Luraville, circa 1882. Local tradition states that the man with the pole is Washington Irvine. *Suwannee County Clerk of Court.*

fire in 1888 and died on December 26 of the same year at the age of fifteen as a result of her wounds. According to one source, she died at the home of Dr. Perry McIntosh, an uncle on her mother's side and a close cousin of her father's. Dr. McIntosh had been Lura's guardian after the 1872 death of her mother and 1882 death of Colonel Irvine. Dr. McIntosh's large two-story home still stands close to Highway 51. Lura's grave is located just upstream of Luraville in the nearby Ivey-McIntosh Cemetery, along with those of her parents and several other relatives.

Among Luraville's early and influential settlers was William B. Telford. Telford was a preacher who arrived in the area in 1864, during the height of the Civil War. Telford Springs, a popular site in the Luraville area, is named after the preacher.

Luraville entered its heyday in 1890, when phosphate was discovered there in January. It was not long before local farmers were digging up their fields with dreams of getting rich. After numerous attempts, it was determined that only the phosphate found around Luraville was of the right kind for marketing purposes. Luraville briefly became a larger community than Live Oak as investors purchased land and established several phosphate companies. The largest company was the Luraville Phosphate Company, established by Thomas I. McIntosh (Dr. Perry McIntosh's brother) in March 1893 with 320 acres.

The establishment of these phosphate mines spurred railroad construction in the Luraville area; until then, the only two ways to get the phosphate to the market was by steamboat on the Suwannee River or to haul it to Live Oak to access the railroads there. Thomas Dowling, Thomas McIntosh and others established or extended existing rail lines to access the phosphate mines. The phosphate could then be shipped more easily to ports, where it would then be taken to Europe, where the majority of phosphate was needed for fertilizer. Steamboats were also used to transport ice to Dr. Perry McIntosh's icehouse in Luraville.

In 1894, the French Phosphate Company entered Luraville to expand its operations beyond central Florida. The Live Oak & Gulf Railway had been established in 1893 to haul phosphate to Live Oak, and the French company used this railroad when it set up operations. Another major Luraville phosphate company was the Ocala and Blue River Phosphate Company. In 1895, over nine thousand tons of phosphate were shipped from Luraville, and in 1896, nearly eleven thousand tons were shipped. However, phosphate operations stopped at the end of 1896, when it was determined that the phosphate had too much iron content, making it useless for its intended purpose. The existing rail lines morphed into general cargo and passenger carriers to provide income. Lumber was especially important during this period.

During the height of the phosphate boom, Luraville was incorporated as a town on September 20, 1895, with twenty-four of its thirty-five qualified electors present. The meeting was held at the public academy in Luraville. At the meeting, R. Lee Waff was elected mayor; Thomas I. McIntosh, John F. McLeod, George W. Telford, W.H. Cox and W.A. Williams were elected aldermen; March C. Renick was elected town clerk; and Leeander M. Ballantine was elected town marshal. Around the time that it was incorporated, Luraville comprised four stores, two churches, a blacksmith shop, a school, cotton gins, turpentine stills and gristmills, with other businesses and churches in the outlying areas.

Phosphate mining picked back up briefly in 1899, only to slack off again later in the year. Despite previous issues with iron content in the area's phosphate, the Mutual Phosphate Company bought up the French Phosphate Company and other companies beginning in 1907 and operated

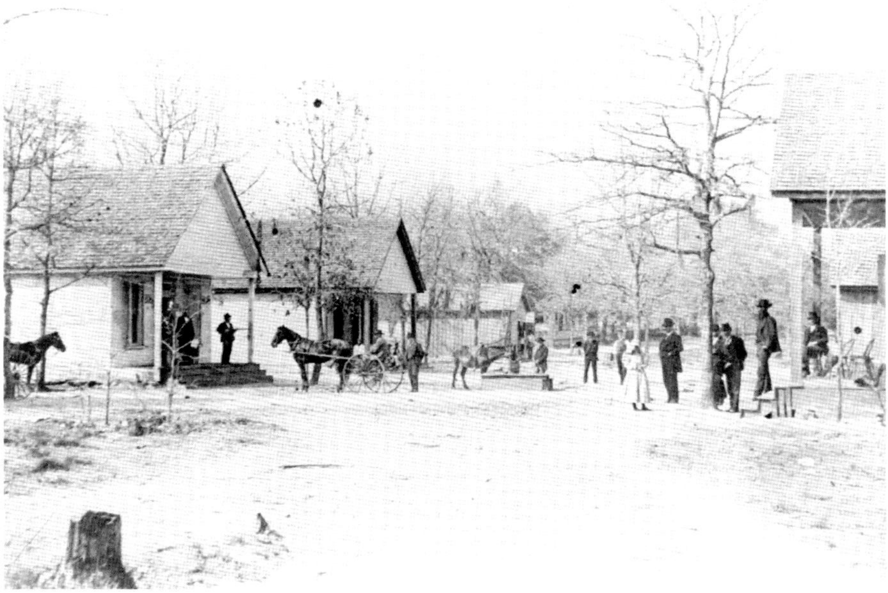

Luraville, circa 1890. The post office is to the right. Note the man with a shotgun on the porch to the left. The second building to the left is the general store of T.I. McIntosh, and the third building to the left is a blacksmith shop. *Advent Christian Village Archives.*

the phosphate mines for nearly a decade. However, the amount mined was nothing like it had been during its heyday of 1895–96. World War I, which began in 1914, finished phosphate mining in the Luraville region; the world powers were too busy fighting to worry about fertilizer from the United States.

Several events brought about the demotion of Luraville in the years immediately prior to, during and after World War I. These include the loss of phosphate mining and associated railroads and the construction of better roads and cars that allowed for farther travel. A metal and wood bridge was built in 1906–7 to replace the ferry first operated by Washington L. Irvine. By 1941, this bridge was in such bad shape that the county commissioners were forced to erect a "cross at your own risk" sign. The next year, the board of county commissioners finally condemned and boarded up the bridge. When the bridge was demolished in 1947, parts were used to repair the equally decrepit Nobles Ferry Bridge (which later fell into the Suwannee River while being crossed by a tractor-trailer). The Hal W. Adams Bridge, built in 1947 as Florida's first suspension span bridge, replaced the old Luraville bridge.

The community of Luraville, without a local government, shrank until it became the quiet, rural settlement that it is today. Within a few miles' drive are numerous local opportunities for cave diving, and its "downtown" area still holds some treasures, such as Dr. Perry McIntosh's home and office.

## OTHER COMMUNITIES

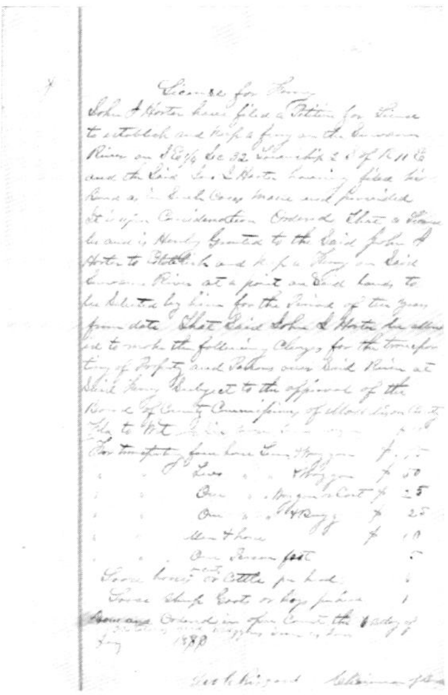

Charges for using John Horton's Ferry at modern-day Dowling Park, 1880. *Suwannee County Clerk of Court.*

Other communities were not as lasting. Before bridges spanned the Suwannee River, ferries operated at various strategic points, connecting one county to another. Small communities usually grew up around these ferries. They included Barrington's Ferry, Levingston's Ferry (near present-day Dowling Park), Charles' Ferry (Charles Springs), Platt's Ferry at Columbus, Rowland's Bluff Ferry (now Branford) and a ferry near Lower Mineral Spring (now Suwannee Springs). Typical charges to ride a ferry in 1872 were $0.10 per foot passenger, $0.25 for a man and horse, $0.50 for a horse and buggy or ox cart, $0.75 for a two-horse wagon, $1.00 for a four-horse wagon and $1.50 for a six-horse wagon. However, once bridges were built to consolidate traffic across the rivers, the ferry crossings closed and the communities around them vanished for the most part.

There were also many communities that arose near major points of travel or natural resources. Cuyler was established in or before 1862 near Live Oak. Fort Izard, halfway between the present-day communities of Luraville and Branford, was also settled in or before 1862, and it is found on at least one map of Suwannee County. Riceville was settled sometime before 1878 at a site exactly two miles north of Luraville. It was named after the Honorable John W. Rice, judge of Suwannee County in 1868.

Padlock was settled in 1873 and named for a convict camp located there. The community was the center of operations for C.K. Dutton and

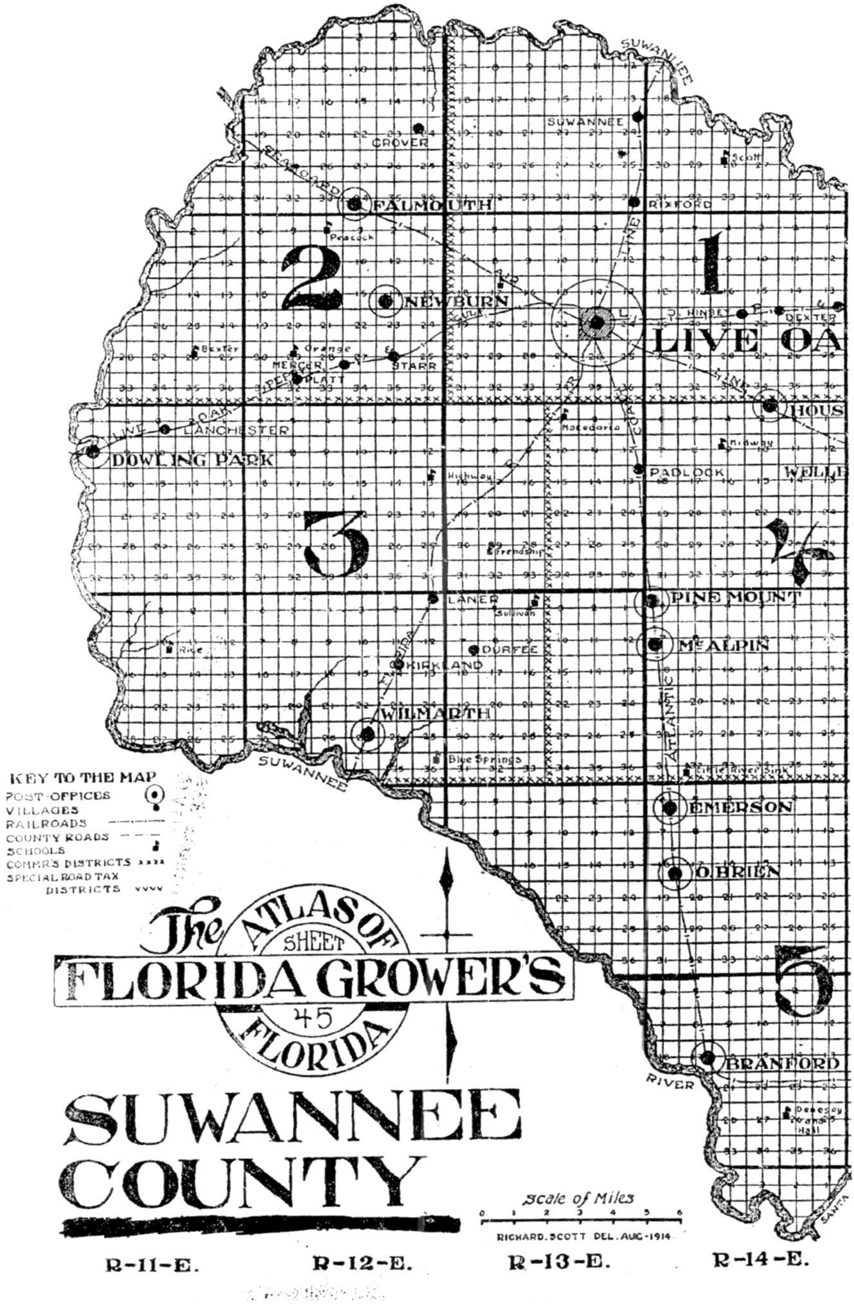


A map of Suwannee County from 1918, showing numerous communities that no longer exist. *Dave Phinney*.

Company (a general stores manufacturer), but agricultural products were also harvested there.

Pinemount was settled in 1883 on the Savannah, Florida & Western Railway. Its population in 1886 and 1887 was two hundred people, with lumber, cotton and vegetables being the main products. At one point in its history, the community boasted three stores, a steam-operated sawmill, a public school and a Baptist church.

Rixford was named for George C. Rixford, naval stores manufacturer and the owner of a sawmill, gristmill, rice mill and cotton gin.

Little River was settled sometime around 1880 east of McAlpin, and its principal products were cotton and vegetables. It should not be confused with the Little River founded by George E. McClellan several miles to the north. The community had a population of seventy-five men, women and children in 1886. It included two sawmills, a gristmill and an academy. It was briefly famous for the "Honey" peaches grown there.

The town of Poplar, east of Ellaville, was a community ultimately doomed by the realization that its products were too far from the markets in Live Oak and other booming towns, a fact noted in 1884 by a traveler.

Wilson was a community seven miles south of O'Brien along the Savannah, Florida & Western Railway. It thrived between 1860 and 1890, when more than sixty families availed themselves of the fruit, cattle and sheep markets located there. Nearby Cypress Lake served as a thirty-acre recreation area in the late 1880s. In 1884, a traveler noted that Wilson had an opening for cotton gins, sawmills and gristmills, and the community was thriving.

By 1900, there were or had been several other small communities in Suwannee County. A casual glance at old maps reveals dozens of forgotten communities. After a decrease in the production of turpentine, lumber and cotton by 1920, along with improvements in transportation and a worldwide depression, these small communities dried up. Little remains of these once-thriving areas other than a few country roads, scattered houses and vanishing relics. For many of these communities, their histories and namesakes have disappeared with them.

# CONCLUSION

Suwannee County is blessed to retain many memorials to those who have gone on before. The county is also fortunate to have many of its older buildings intact, showing the small-town charm that so many Americans desire. Some ways of life have not changed much in two hundred years, as the rural county continues its export of a variety of crops.

However, times have indeed changed. The lives of countless influential and ordinary citizens have been forgotten in the hustle and bustle of modern life. The once-grand steamboats that sailed up and down the Suwannee River are long gone, replaced by personal watercraft far less majestic in appearance. The whistle of numerous locomotives making their way through the vast virgin woods has been replaced by automobiles, aircraft and subdivisions.

Despite these changes, the dark Suwannee River still flows lazily toward the Gulf of Mexico, as it has for thousands of years. Those who visit or live in Suwannee County still find themselves way down upon the Suwannee River....

# BIBLIOGRAPHY


Bass, Bob. *When Steamboats Reigned in Florida*. Gainesville: University Press of Florida, 2008.

City of Live Oak. City Council Minute Books. Live Oak, Florida.

Douglass High School Alumni & Historical Association, Inc. *Douglass Center Briefing and Information Packet*, 2017. Live Oak, Florida.

Georgia's Railroad History and Heritage. http://www.railga.com.

*Live Oak Daily Democrat*. Live Oak Florida, 1906.

Musgrove, Eric. *Reflections of Suwannee County*. Live Oak, FL: Eric Musgrove Books, 2008.

Powell, J.C. *American Siberia; or, Fourteen Years' Experience in a Southern Convict Camp*. Chicago: W.B. Conkey Company, 1891.

State Library and Archives of Florida, Photographic Collection. http://www.floridamemory.com/PhotographicCollection.

Suwannee County Board of County Commissioners. *Suwannee County Centennial 1858–1958 Souvenir Program*. Live Oak, FL: Suwannee County Board of County Commissioners, 1958.

Suwannee County Clerk of the Circuit Court. Live Oak, Florida.

Suwannee County Historical Museum. Live Oak, Florida.

Suwannee County School Board. Live Oak, Florida.

*Suwannee Democrat*. Live Oak, Florida. Various years.

Suwannee 2000 History Committee. *Echoes of the Past: A History of Suwannee County, 1858–2000*. St. Petersburg, FL: Southern Heritage Press, 2000.

Turner, Gregg. *Making of America: A Short History of Florida Railroads*. Charleston, SC: Arcadia Publishing, 2003.

# INDEX

## T



## U



## W

# ABOUT THE AUTHOR

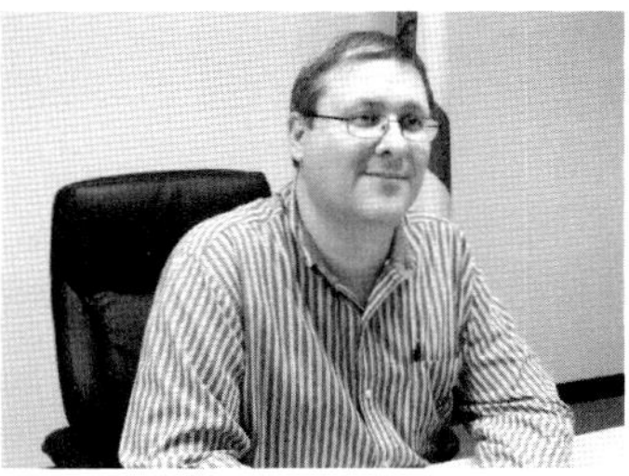

The author, 2016. *Author's collection.*

Eric Musgrove is a seventh-generation native of Suwannee County, Florida. Growing up on the family's country homestead, he quickly developed a love for history that has remained strong throughout his life. The 1996 salutatorian of Suwannee High School, Eric was also a December 1997 valedictorian of Montgomery, Alabama's Faulkner University, where he received a bachelor of science degree in history at the age of nineteen. Returning home to Suwannee County in 1998, Eric began working for the Suwannee County Clerk of the Court's Office. He remains there today as historian and records manager, among many other duties.

Eric has been the youngest member of the Suwannee County Historical Commission since he was appointed to it in 2003. He was treasurer from 2008 to 2014 and since October 2014 has served as its chairman. Eric is a frequent presenter of local history and has been mentioned in the *New York Times*, *Washington Post* and *Chicago Tribune*, among hundreds of other prominent national and international newspapers. In early 2012, Eric was awarded the 2011 Trailblazer Award by the Suwannee County Chamber of Commerce in recognition of his work in preserving and presenting local history. Since 2013, he has also published a weekly historical column for one of Suwannee County's local newspapers, the *Suwannee Democrat*.

Eric married his college sweetheart, Sarah, in 1998, and they live near Live Oak on part of the old family homestead with their two children, Alex and Abby. Eric has authored four published books: *Reflections of Suwannee County*, *Suwannee Memories*, *There Let Me Live and Die* and *Images of America: Suwannee County*.